Updated

Knowledge Lighthouse

A SKILL-BASED COURSE ON GENERAL KNOWLEDGE

8

Name : ....

Grade: .... Section : ....

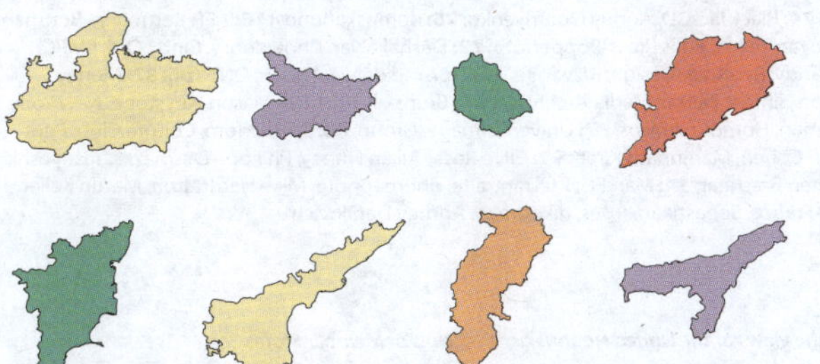

India has 28 states and 8 union territories. Can you identify these states?

Seema Chari • Kunal Savarkar

HarperCollins*Publishers*

Publishing operations in 17 countries and 120+ imprints globally

William Collins' dream of knowledge for all began with the publication of his first book in 1819. A self-educated mill worker, he not only enriched millions of lives, but also founded a flourishing publishing house. Today, staying true to this spirit, Collins books are packed with inspiration, innovation and practical expertise. They place you at the centre of a world of possibility and give you exactly what you need to explore it.

Published by Collins Learning
An imprint of HarperCollins*Publishers* India
Building No. 10, Tower A, 4th Floor, DLF Cyber City, Gurugram, Haryana 122002, India

First edition: 2025
Reprint: 10 9 8 7 6 5 4 3 2 1
ISBN: 978-93-6213-000-6

Artwork, typesetting and layout by **Toon Fantasy and Majik Strokes, GNZE Interactions**
Printed and bound in India by MicroPrints India, New Delhi

ACKNOWLEDGEMENTS

Cover and title page images: Anastasiia Ovsiannykova

Inside: Icons: Hiranmay Baidya, LvNL, cienpies, KaanC; **3:** impulse50; **4:** Natalia Darmoroz, impulse50, ONYXprj; **5:** Natalia Darmoroz, ONYXprj, Magnilion, colematt; **6:** Natwwwalia Darmoroz, impulse50, ONYXprj; **8:** Natalia Darmoroz, impulse50, ONYXprj; **9:** Vikeriya; **10:** ZU_09, Archive Photos, Frank Trapper, clu; **11:** raclro, Robertus Pudyanto, BAY ISMOYO, VCG; **12:** fatido, DNY59, t_kimura, anand purohit, Rewat-Wannasuk, Simeon VD, Urfan Dadashov, kolae; **13:** avid_creative, AYImages, yesfoto, luismmolina, Tomekbudujedomek; **14:** Bettmann, Jonathan Leibson, Leonardo Cendamo, David Levenson, Will Ragozzino, Gilbert Carrasquillo, NicolÃ² Campo; **16:** Phototreat, R.M. Nunes, Eva-Katalin, mingurl kim, Oleh_Slobodeniuk; **17:** Sproetniek, fototrav, focusstock, Ozbalci, fotoVoyager; **18:** Subhendu Sarkar, Bloomberg; **19:** JP Yim, Luca Teuchmann; **20:** fotoember, f9photos, Mitesh_kothari; **21:** Bloomberg, saiko3p, reddees; **22:** Justin Sullivan, Charley Gallay, Mail Today, Fotosearch, Bettmann; **23:** Antonio Scorza, Hindustan Times, Noam Galai; Dan Kitwood, Popperfoto, **27:** Society Picture Library, duncan1890, **29:** The India Today Group, Mint, NurPhoto, Chandan Khanna, Sopa; **30:** MarekSzandurski, Mail Today, Pool, danefromspain, Sebastian Widmann, Panupong Changchai, Heritage Images, The Asahi Shimbun, Stock Ninja Studio, Leontura, Kamlesh Suthar; **31:** pilesasmiles, fbxx; **32:** LordRunar, ZU_09, pioneer111, ekolara, CHIARI_VFX; **33:** traveler1116, duncan1890, dem10, xur82, Witthaya Prasongsin; **34:** Jeff Rotman, xxmmxx, eli_asenova, OGphoto, SongayeNovell, MediaNews Group/Orange County; **35:** reptiles4all, Adam-Springer, wrangel, aluxum, Stan Tekiela, Ken Griffiths, Insight Imaging; **36:** Sjo, BardoczPeter, Rudimencial, Hulton Deutsch, desifoto, NurPhoto; **37:** joeravi, f9photos; **38:** DorianGray, penguenstok, Nerthuz, Kate Smith, alexandr_1958; **39:** SpiffyJ, brightstars, Yuri_Arcurs; **40:** piotr_malczyk, Jadezmith, subjug, Ligrenok; **41:** Getty Images; **42:** Nataliia Prachova, Dmitry Kovalchuk, ProVectors, Stefan Ilic, Sofir, LeventKonuk, adamkaz, code6d; **43:** PRAKASH SINGH, SOPA Images, SOPA Images, Balaji Srinivasan; **44:** Rhona Wise, Stan Honda, alexsl, vchal; **45:** AFP, Mark Brake, metamorworks; **46:** f9photos, Global_Pics, yulkapopkova, Nilesh Shah, Wei Hao Ho; **47:** Deep Pai, Â© Vincent Boisvert, rajatk, Chaithanya Krishna Photography, Satvik Shahapur, Emilija Manevska; **48:** zodebala, f11photo, Suprabhat Dutta; **49:** kickstand, Pgiam, Deejpilot; **50:** Dinodia Photos, Mail Today, Thomas Imo, Hindustan Times; **51:** Tim Sloan, Hulton Archive, Michael Ochs Archives , Dave Benett; **52:** AROYBARMAN, skynesher, Tamar Mirianashvili, Rizky Panuntun; **53:** John S Lander, wind-moon, oleg66, wanderluster, JeremyRichards, Dea Picture Library, Sovfoto, traveler1116, Pallava Bagla; **54:** ullstein bild Dtl., Pallava Bagla; **55:** Pgiam; **57:** Universal History Archive, Dea Picture Library, pictore; **58:** Mark Davis, Kevin Mazur, Manny Carabel, Kevin Winter, CBS Photo Archive, Dimitrios Kambouris; **59:** Kevin Mazur, Axelle/Bauer-Griffin, Jon Kopaloff, Randy Shropshire, Mike Marsland, Gareth Cattermole; **62:** f9photos, Nisha_images, Kaushik Ghosh, MartinMachnowski, Muralinath, Anna Egorova; Vinayak Jagtap, **63:** Noah Seelam, Saumil Shah, SoumenNath, SJPailkar, David Talukdar, webphotographeer; **64:** shutswis, pixdeluxe, lamyai, Artur Didyk; **65:** microgen, amriphoto, peepo, Duncan_Andison, Tim Clayton - Corbis; **66:** narvikk, Sheridan Libraries/Levy/Gado; **67:** Yvonne Hemsey, De Agostini Picture Library, Lmpc; **68:** Imagno, Gallo Images, Bettmann; **69:** Stock Montage, Stephen F. Somerstein, Hulton Deutsch, ilbusca, Paras Griffin; **70:** John Lamparski, urbanbuzz, nicescene, CTRPhotos, Gabe Ginsberg; **71:** Evan Agostini, Yvonne Hemsey, awiekupo, CTRPhotos, Ricardo DeAratanha; **72:** Sebastian D'souza, Pacific Press, STR, Historical; **73:** AmandaLewis, Imagno, Sjo; **74:** BlackJack3D, Andriy Onufriyenko; **75:** domoskanonos; **76:** AFP, Bettmann, Bettmann, Mint; **77:** Bert Hardy / Stringer, PASCAL GEORGE, Boston Globe / Contributor, ullstein bild, Hindustan Times, Rolls Press/Popperfoto; **79:** Deshakalyan Chowdhury, Cindy Ord, LMPC, LMPC, LMPC; **80:** marinapron, Stock Ninja Studio, Tetiana Lazunova, Ruslan Fazlulov; **81:** tilo, Ivcandy, RedKoalaDesign, Rizvan3d, Avector, md delwar hosen, ONYXprj; **82:** Money Sharma; **83:** Tim Graham, Jeff Overs, Â°XPÂ°; **84:** Central Press / Stringer, Universal , Pool Francolon/Simon, Fairfax Media Archives, Clive Brunskill; **85:** Clive Mason, Keystone, New York Times Co., Clive Rose, Emmanuel Dunand; **86:** Dea / G. Dagli Orti, Dea / G. Dagli Orti, Werner Forman, HomoCosmicos; **87:** UniversalImagesGroup; **88:** Popperfoto, Culture Club, Print Collector; **89:** Professional Sport; **90:** Punit Paranjpe, Hindustan Times; **91:** Hindustan Times, Yvan Cohen, Manjunath Kiran; **92:** Clive Rose, Julian Finney, Philippe Desmazes, Yasuyoshi Chiba, Kyodo News; **93:** Bloomberg, Boston Globe, Bloomberg, The AGE, Monica Schipper, Stephen Brashear; **94:** MarkFGD, ferrantraite, ghornephoto, Mike Harrington, Martin Keiler; **95:** Justin Sullivan, Bettmann, simonkr; **96:** yuri4u80, powerofforever, mikroman6; **97:** Keystone-France, Sebastiaan Kroes, dikobraziy, Andrey Danilovich

SDG logo and icons: https://www.un.org/sustainabledevelopment/

Browse the complete Collins catalogue at www.collins.in.
For any queries/feedback, please write to us at SCHOOLSUPPORT@harpercollins.co.in.

Preface

Like the universe, knowledge, too, is limitless. No matter how much we know, there is always more to know. In the 21st century, thanks to the leaps that technology has made and continues to make, we shall have to gather knowledge throughout our lives; so much so that we have coined a new portmanteau, to describe it: 'upskilling'.

Another novelty of the third millennium is how we access and absorb knowledge. Apart from human sources (family, teachers, friends), there are the online ones (website, social media). Yet, despite all this easy availability and accessibility, it is not always easy to distinguish between real and fake, relevant and redundant, significant and inconsequential.

Updated Knowledge Lighthouse is a series meant for GenZ, that is, learners born after Y2K. The series covers 'classic' general knowledge content for learners of grades 1 to 8, but lays special emphasis on skills —learning skills, literacy skills and life skills— as well as knowledge gleaned from new learnings of the past few years, from COVID-19 to sustainability, from data science to global issues in an ever-shifting, ever-ephemeral, post-information world. All the new chapters, although dealing with topics of great gravity, are presented in an age-appropriate and friendly manner so as to kindle interest and lay the foundation for more in-depth learning.

A critical component of the Updated Knowledge Lighthouse books is the India content, wherein our country in all its complexity and diversity is presented through colourful, simple and exciting tasks, plus brand-new features such as state-focus, city-focus and visit-a-monument.

A particularly career-friendly inclusion in the Updated Knowledge Lighthouse series is Science, technology, engineering and mathematics (STEM), the disciplines of the future, and new global issues, presented under World Today. We hope to lighten these subjects for students, by adding a little sprinkle of trivia to them.

Sustainable development is one of the key phrases of this millennium, but what does it really mean for us, especially for children? The all-new Life on Land and Climate Action chapters not only sensitise learners but also encourage direct and immediate action.

In the Skills pages, the life skills section has tasks on safety and self-awareness. Connecting the dots is the foundation of knowledge and the series has chapters based on Higher Order Thinking Skills (HOTS) and critical thinking to train young minds to see patterns, learn to eliminate or choose details and observe better.

Become a Champion Quizzer

Updated Knowledge Lighthouse encourages all learners to be curious and explore the world around them. Those who observe and absorb all the time, learn from everyone and everything; they are the ones who become quizzers. Here are six rules that will help you become a champion quizzer.

1. Be curious—look around you, see everything, read everything.
2. Listen to others.
3. Seek out new experiences.
4. Learn to link events and people.
5. Do your own research and learn to spot fake news.
6. Remember, no matter how much you know, there is much more that you have yet to learn.

Now, go for it! We are sure that this series will expose a whole new generation of learners to the fun universe of general knowledge and enhance their love for learning and discovery.

~ Seema Chari and Kunal Savarkar

In this series ...

Updated Knowledge Lighthouse tasks are thematic and linear with visual, verbal, and strategic inputs to help students solve them and acquire knowledge through a wide range of subjects and themes.

World Around Us

7 Countries of the World

Solve the clues to find the names of countries using words from the help box. To further help you, the last letters of the names have been provided.

1 This country has wonderful mountain peaks and is famous for its banking system and its precision watch-making. ....D

2 Genghis Khan, the famous ruler, was from this country and Buddhism is its largest religion.

World Around Us tasks take the learners on an exciting journey across the world.

Natural World

18 Self-Defence in Animals

Every living being in nature has evolved defence mechanisms to protect itself from p

Match the animal with the defence mechanism it uses by writing the correct number in the boxes.

1 Bee — a Displays a pattern of large eyes on its wing surface to scare the attacker

2 Octopus — b Lies still as if it is dead, in the presence

Natural World section uncovers the magical realm of plants, animals and birds.

Life on Land

23 Plastic

In any "Save Earth" discussion, one of the biggest villains is plastic. Plastic has been around for a little more than a century, and modern living is impossible without it. But everyone knows that it is bad for our environment.

Read the text and complete the story of plastic with words from the help box. Watch out, as there are 12 blanks and 16 answers!

1 Plastic mostly comes from petroleum or natural gas, which are both .... The word plastic comes from the Greek word *plastikos* means "that which can be .... or moulded".

2 In fact, apart from being flexible, plastic is ...., durable and cheap to produce, which is why it is so popular.

Sustainable Development Goals sensitises learners towards sustainable development of the planet.

India Focus

24 What's in a Train Name?

Use the clues and help box to fill in the terminus of each train mentioned below.

1 The Black Diamond Express connects coal-mining cities in East-Central India. It runs from Howrah to ....

2 *Thirukkural* was written by Thiruvalluvar, whose statue is found at the southern of the Indian subcontinent. The Thirukkural Express runs from Hazrat Nizamu to ....

3 *Maitree* means 'friendship'. The Maitree Express is the first passenger railway link between Bangladesh and India (since 1965) and links Kolkata to ....

India Focus tasks are created to evoke a sense of wonder and pride in our nation.

Art and Entertainment

34 That's My Music!

When you enjoy the music of an artist or band, you try to listen to everything they've created.

Match each set of songs with the musician or band.

1 *Roar* / *Chained to the Rhythm* / *Firework* — a Justin Bieber

2 *Gorgeous* / *You Belong With Me* / *Blank Space* — b Demi Lovato

Art and Entertainment tasks celebrate artists, artworks, paintings, movies, awards and achievements.

STEM

38 Science of Sports

Sports equipment and techniques are based on science.

Use the pictures and match Column A to Column B to complete the statements.

Column A	Column B
1 In baseball, metal bats help the ball travel faster, but wooden bats continue to be used	a That's why it is small and has dimples on it.

Sports section provides rules and records related to different sports.

Language and Literature

40 Immortal Words

Some speeches are remembered and quoted decades or even centuries after they were made.

Match the speakers with their immortal words.

1 Queen Elizabeth I — a In May 1941, a Nobel laureate from India on his eightieth birthday said, "As I look around I see the crumbling ruins of a proud civilisation strewn like a vast heap of futility."

b In April 1917, at the first anniversary of

Language and Literature tasks present vocabulary and etymology in a fun way.

World Today

19 Social Movements of the 21st Century

As we mark the silver jubilee of this century, we can see that people of the twent are more vocal than ever before, and members of every community have increa a public voice through mass movements. Some of these are triggered by immedi while others have been simmering for a while before finding expression. Match movements with their description and write the name of the country in which t

Name	Description
1 Jasmine Revolution/ Arab Spring	a Led by social activist Anna Hazare, this 2011 movemen saw protests across the country by citizens fighting against widespread corruption.
2 Schools Strike for Climate	b This 2011 movement led to people talking about economic inequality and corporate greed; and the impact of wealth on law-making in the world's richest country.

Word Today highlights the importance of understanding and addressing global challenges together.

Whiz fact

According to NASA, it takes astronauts 45 minutes to put on a spacesuit, but it protects them from temperature as low as -150° to a high temperature of upto 135°.

Whiz Fact is a spin-off fact about each topic or theme.

STEM

31 Space Exploration

For as long as humans have existed, space has played an important part in our lives. Early man navigated paths across land and oceans using the stars.

Use the clues and pictures to solve the crossword relating to the history of space exploration.

STEM highlights some scientific achievements and provides facts for others.

Whiz quiz

Find out the answers and fill in the blanks about India's recent space achievement.

The .... launched .... from the .... on 22 July 2019. It consists of a lunar orbiter, a lander and a lunar rover called .... Developed entirely in India, the main scientific objective of the mission is to map the location and abundance of .... It landed on ...., 6 September 2019.

Whiz Quiz are fun activities that encourage self-learning.

21st Century Skills

21st century skills are necessary to succeed in the Age of Information. These skills are divided into three main sets, namely, learning skills, literacy skills and life skills.

Learning Skills

- Critical Thinking and HOTS
- Creativity
- Collaboration
- Communication

Learning Skills

14 Startups Around Us

In the last 20 years or so, new companies, popularly known as startups, have used technology to change the way we live, travel, eat and shop.

Use the fun clues to get the names of 11 such brands and solve the crossword below.

Literacy Skills

- Technology
- Information
- Media
- Financial Literacy
- Data Handling

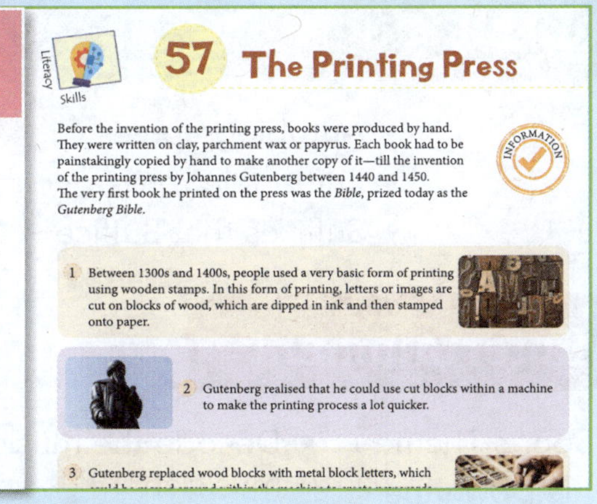

Literacy Skills

57 The Printing Press

Before the invention of the printing press, books were produced by hand. They were written on clay, parchment wax or papyrus. Each book had to be painstakingly copied by hand to make another copy of it—till the invention of the printing press by Johannes Gutenberg between 1440 and 1450. The very first book he printed on the press was the *Bible*, prized today as the *Gutenberg Bible*.

1 Between 1300s and 1400s, people used a very basic form of printing using wooden stamps. In this form of printing, letters or images are cut on blocks of wood, which are dipped in ink and then stamped onto paper.

2 Gutenberg realised that he could use cut blocks within a machine to make the printing process a lot quicker.

3 Gutenberg replaced wood blocks with metal block letters, which

Life Skills

- Problem-solving
- Self-awareness
- Safety
- Social Skills

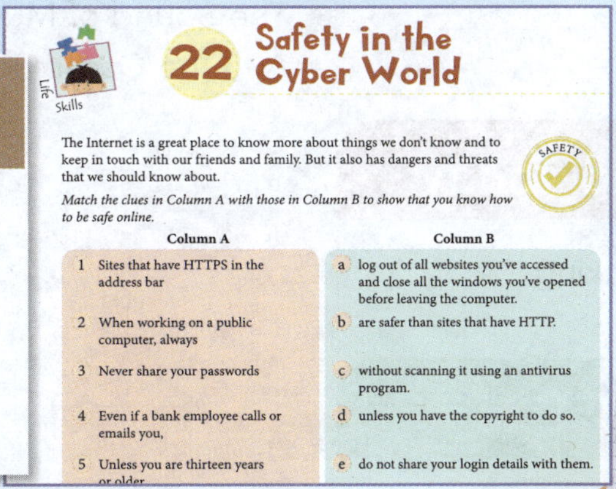

Life Skills

22 Safety in the Cyber World

The Internet is a great place to know more about things we don't know and to keep in touch with our friends and family. But it also has dangers and threats that we should know about.

Match the clues in Column A with those in Column B to show that you know how to be safe online.

Column A	Column B
1 Sites that have HTTPS in the address bar	a log out of all websites you've accessed and close all the windows you've opened before leaving the computer.
2 When working on a public computer, always	b are safer than sites that have HTTP.
3 Never share your passwords	c without scanning it using an antivirus program.
4 Even if a bank employee calls or emails you,	d unless you have the copyright to do so.
5 Unless you are thirteen years or older	e do not share your login details with them.

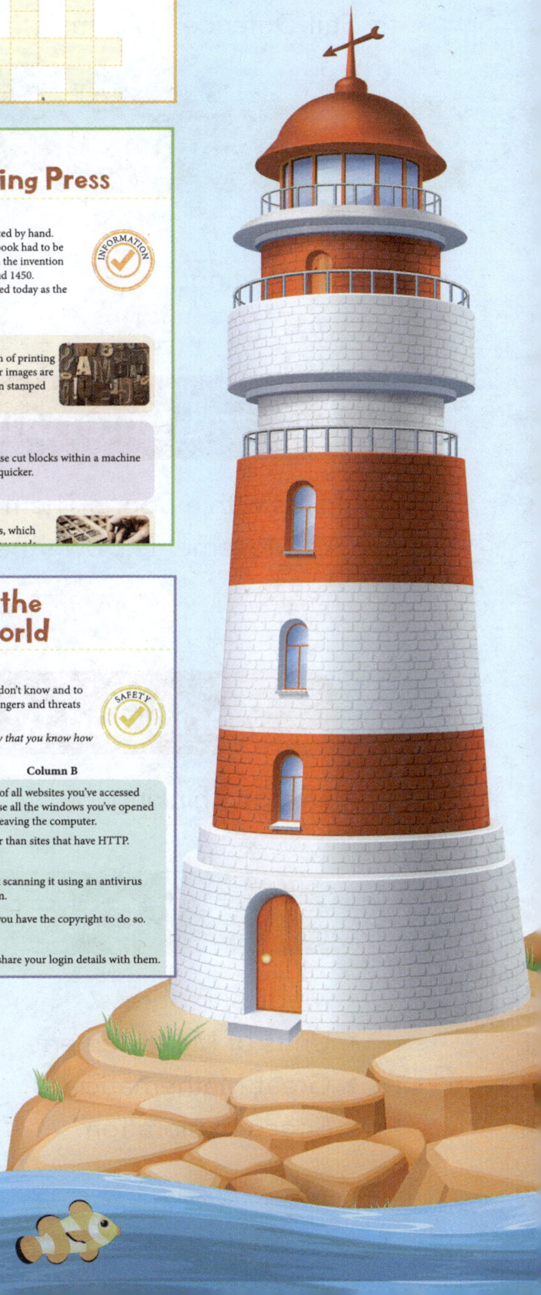

Detailed Contents

Contents

1 Super Sleuths

Detectives use clues to solve mysteries.

Read the description clues and unscramble the highlighted letters to compose the names of the detectives.

1. Agatha Christie created this Belgian detective whose most regular sidekick is Captain Arthur Hastings.
2. This teenage girl detective features in books written by multiple authors under the pseudonym Carolyn C Keene.
3. Arthur Conan Doyle created this remarkable character whose adventures are mostly narrated by John H Watson.
4. Satyajit Ray created this detective who is helped by his cousin Topshe and friend Jatayu.
5. Sharadindu Bandyopadhyay made this Chinabazar, Kolkata-based Bengali detective who is a truth-seeker and prefers to be called *Satyanweshi*.
6. Publisher Edward Stratemeyer created these All-American jeans-clad boy detectives , usually written under the pseudonym Franklin W Dixon.

and

Whiz fact

Detective stories or murder mysteries, also called whodunnits (who done it?), are a recent genre of writing. One of the first fictional detectives was C. Auguste Dupin, a character created by Edgar Allan Poe, in a grimly named novel called *The Murders in the Rue Morgue*, who inspired the personalities of both Holmes and Poirot.

Learning Skills

2 Numbers in Names

CRITICAL THINKING

The answer to each of these clues is a number. Choose the correct number using the help box and fill in the blanks.

1 Phileas Fogg and his valet Passepartout circumnavigated the globe in *Around the World in* .... *Days* written by Jules Verne.

2 Alexandre Dumas authored the novel *The* .... *Musketeers* with the titular characters Athos, Porthos and Aramis.

3 American rapper and singer Curtis James Jackson III is better known by his stage name .... Cent.

4 .... *Hours* is a biographical survival film based on true events about a man who was trapped in a canyon for over six days and how he survived.

5 Gabriel Garcia Marquez's famous novel .... *Years of Solitude*, originally written in Spanish, is a tale of seven generations of the Buendia family.

6 Stanley Kubrick directed the famous 1968 science fiction film inspired by a short story written by Arthur C Clarke, called .... : *A Space Odyssey*.

7 'Summer of ....' is a song co-written by Bryan Adams. It was recorded for his 1984 album, *Reckless*.

8 Scheherazade is the storyteller of .... *Nights*.

Help box

2001	*'69*	*One Hundred*	*Eighty*
50	*One Thousand and One*	*Three*	*127*

Whiz fact

Jules Verne's science fiction novel, Twenty Thousand Leagues Under the Sea refers to the distance, not depth, travelled. This journey covered 20,000 metric leagues, or almost 80,000 km, which is roughly twice the circumference of the Earth.

Sports

3 The Asian Games

The Asian Games are a continental multi-sport event held every four years among athletes from all over Asia.

Choose the correct answers.

1 The 1982 Asian Games were held in New Delhi/Jakarta.

2 China/Thailand is the only country to have hosted the Asian Games four times.

3 The first Asiad to have a mascot was the 1982 Asian Games, New Delhi/1986 Asian Games, Seoul.

4 1994 was the first time that Asian Games were hosted by a city other than the national capital. This Asiad was hosted in Hiroshima/Osaka.

5 2014/2018 was the first time the Asian Games took place in more than one city.

6 In 1994, the Asian Games included Kazakhstan/Macau for the first time.

7 Palestine/Israel participated in the Asian Games from 1954 to 1974, but is now excluded because of political reasons.

8 India/China has competed in all editions of the Asian Games.

9 The Asian Games are designed to promote understanding and friendship/industry between Asian countries.

10 The 1986 Asiad was held in Seoul in North Korea/South Korea.

Whiz quiz

Only seven countries have participated in all editions of the Asian Games. Do you know them? Write their names here.

....

....

Literacy Skills

4 Universal Symbols

A symbol is a mark, sign or word that indicates, signifies or is understood as representing an idea, object or relationship.

Use the images and the words from the help box to fill in the blanks.

1 The .... trademark symbol provides notice that the symbol has been legally registered to represent a company or product.

2 The .... mark is used to indicate that something is correct, verified or completed.

3 The .... symbol came about when the words 'on' and 'off' were replaced by the numbers 1 and 0. Later on, the numeric symbols were superimposed onto each other.

4 The .... symbol was designed as the logo for the Direct Action Committee against Nuclear War. Today, it is popular all over the world.

5 The .... is the international symbol of breast cancer awareness. It expresses moral support for women with breast cancer and represents health, vitality and empowerment of women.

6 The .... symbol was originally a symbol of good fortune and means 'well-being' in Sanskrit.

7 The Maltese .... is used in various entities, including the Maltese civil ensign, Malta's national airline Air Malta and in military and civil orders around the world.

Help box

swastika | peace | registered | pink ribbon | cross | tick | power

Whiz fact

Bluetooth technology was named after an ancient Danish King Harald (known as Harald Blåtand or 'Bluetooth') because he was known for uniting various kingdoms together, similar to how Bluetooth technology connects multiple devices.

STEM

5 Medical Progress

Breakthroughs in medicine over the past century have resulted in better diagnosis and better treatment of diseases.

Use the clues and help box to fill in the blanks.

1 In 1921, Frederick Banting and Charles Best discovered ...., a hormone which if not produced or produced in low quantities, causes diabetes.

2 In 1931, Ernst Ruska and Max Knoll invented the .... microscope which helped doctors see bacteria and viruses clearly for the first time.

3 In 1952, Jonas Salk developed the first effective ....vaccine.

4 In 1953, Leroy Stevens discovered .... which are now used to grow new tissues and organs in humans.

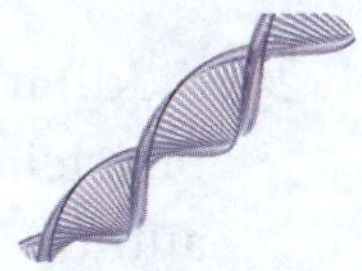

5 In 1953, Francis Crick and James Watson discovered the structure of ...., which explained how characteristics were inherited from parents' cells.

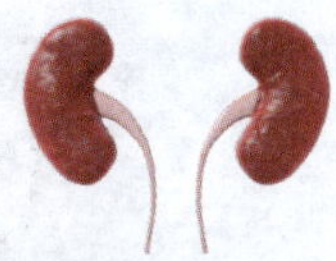

6 Dr. Joseph Murray conducted the first .... transplant in 1956.

7 In 1967, cardiac surgeon Dr. Christiaan Barnard performed the first ever .... transplant.

8 In 1978, Patrick Steptoe used in vitro fertility treatment to create the world's first .... baby.

9 Scottish researchers Ian Wilmut, Keith Campbell and their colleagues bred the first cloned sheep called .... in 1996.

Help box

DNA	Dolly	electron	heart	insulin
kidney	polio	stem cells	test tube	

Whiz fact

In the 1800s, scientists discovered that nitrous oxide helps to relieve pain, but it wasn't widely used by dentists till the 1860s. It is nicknamed 'laughing gas' because it makes people happy, thereby making them laugh. Using nitrous oxide is a safe and effective way to relax before any procedure.

6 Prizes for Writing

Some of the most prestigious awards that some very talented Indians (or people of Indian origin) have won for writing include the Booker Prize, the Pulitzer Prize, the Sahitya Akademi Award, the Jnanpith Award and of course, the Nobel Prize in Literature.

Match these writers, their works and awards for their expert wielding of the pen.

Writer	Description of work	Award
1 Rabindranath Tagore 	i His first book called *The Emperor of All Maladies: A Biography of Cancer*, hailed as "an elegant inquiry, both clinical and personal, into a the long history of an insidious disease."	a Man Booker Prize, 2006
2 Siddhartha Mukherjee, physician, biologist, author 	ii Along with two other reporters of BuzzFeed News, she used satellite imagery, architectural expertise, and several interviews with former prisoners, to unveil vast infrastructures for the detention of minority communities in China.	b Nobel Prize in Literature, 1913
3 Kiran Desai, novelist 	iii His collection of poems translated into English as "Song Offerings" described as "profoundly sensitive, fresh and beautiful".	c Pulitzer Prize for International Reporting, 2021
4 Megha Rajagopalan, reporter 	iv Her second novel, *The Inheritance of Loss*, won numerous accolades for depicting, with much sensitivity, a slew of contemporary themes, like migration, multiculturalism, globalisation, fundamentalism and terrorism.	d Pulitzer Prize for General Non-Fiction, 2011

5 Salman Rushdie, novelist

6 Mahesh Dattani, playwright

7 Amitav Ghosh, fiction and non-fiction writer

8 Aravind Adiga, novelist

v From his first works *The Circle of Reason* and *The Shadow Lines* to *The Ibis Trilogy* to more recent non-fiction works, such as *The Nutmeg's Curse: Parables for a Planet in Crisis*, his works span history, the Indian Ocean and climate change.

vi His *The White Tiger*, written in the Bildungsroman style, traces the life of the protagonist from childhood through to adulthood.

vii *Final Solutions and Other Plays* is a collection of plays that explore themes as diverse as gender identity and politics, family matters, fundamentalism and urban life. It was the first drama collection to win this award in English.

viii His magic realism novel *Midnight's Children* was about a child born on 15 August 1947, whose magic connection with all other children born at the stroke of the midnight hour drives the story.

e Sahitya Akademi Award, 1998

f Booker Prize, 2008

g Man Booker Prize in 1981, Booker of Bookers in 1993 and Best of the Booker 2008

h Jnanpith Award, 2018

Whiz fact

Geetanjali Shree is a Hindi novelist and short story writer living in New Delhi. Her 2018 novel *Ret Samadhi*, translated into English as *Tomb of Sand* by Daisy Rockwell, won the International Booker Prize 2022, the first Hindi novel in translation to receive such an honour.

7 Countries of the World

Solve the clues to find the names of countries using words from the help box. To further help you, the last letters of the names have been provided.

1 This country has wonderful mountain peaks and is famous for its banking system and its precision watch-making.

.... D

2 Genghis Khan, the famous ruler, was from this country and Buddhism is its largest religion.

.... A

3 This African nation is the newest country in the world. Its capital is Juba.

.... H .... N

4 The smallest country in the world by area and population, it is headed by the Pope.

.... N .... Y

5 This South American country is sandwiched between Brazil and Argentina.

.... Y

6 The Kalahari Desert forms a major part of this country. It also has the highest number of African elephants and is the world's largest diamond producing country in terms of value.

.... A

7 The capital of this country is bisected by the river Danube. The inventor of the Rubik's Cube belonged to this country.

.... Y

8 This country is renowned for its ancient cities like Samarkand, Tashkent and Bukhara.

.... N

9 This country is located mainly in the Himalayas but also includes parts of the Indo-Gangetic plain. It became a secular republic in 2008, before which it was a Hindu monarchy.

.... L

10 This Southeast Asian country is traversed by the Mekong river and known for its mountainous terrain, French colonial architecture and Buddhist monasteries.

.... S

Help box

Hungary | Laos | Mongolia | Switzerland | Botswana
South Sudan | Uzbekistan | Vatican City | Nepal | Paraguay

Whiz fact

A country landlocked by another country is called an enclaved country. There are just three enclaved countries in the world—Lesotho surrounded by South Africa, San Marino surrounded by Italy and the Vatican City situated within Rome in Italy.

India Focus

8 Bustling Bengaluru

Bengaluru's leafy avenues and lush green spaces have given it the moniker 'Garden City'. Thanks to its booming IT industry, which attracts the best talent from around the world, it is also called the 'Silicon Valley of India'.

Read the clues about Bengaluru, find the answers in the help box and fill in the blanks. But watch out! There are some extra incorrect answers in the help box.

1. Bengaluru's green lung ....
2. Jamsetji Tata's gift to science research ....
3. Seat of the state government ....
4. The 'Sholay' village! ....
5. Heroic founder of Bengaluru after whom its airport is named ....
6. Bengaluru's metro, dubbed 'our' metro ....
7. Fighter aircraft are 'Made in India' here! ....
8. The 'fragrant' name for the Kannada film industry ....
9. IT firm founded by N. R. Narayan Murthy and six others ....
10. Bengaluru was first made capital of this state in 1947 ....

Help box

Kempegowda | HAL | Namma | Karnataka | NASA | Vidhana Soudha | Kollywood | Mysore | Ramgarh | Ramanagara | IISc | Infosys | Lalbagh Botanical Garden | Sandalwood | Tipu Sultan

Whiz fact

In 2014, Bangalore was officially renamed Bengaluru, following the Kannada pronunciation. The name is either a reference to the Indian *kino* tree, a heroic stone, the city of guards or a plate of boiled beans!

9 Films with a Sports Theme

Match the names of the sports films in Column A with their clues in Column B.

Column A	Column B
1 *Sultan*	a Mahavir Phogat trains his young daughters to become wrestling champions.
2 *Gold*	b Priyanka Chopra plays the part of an Olympic medal winning boxer.
3 *Dangal*	c A wrestler's professional success creates a rift in his personal life.
4 *Lagaan*	d Farhan Akhtar played the title role in this movie based on the life of the athlete called the 'Flying Sikh'.
5 *Paan Singh Tomar*	e Aamir Khan plays Bhuvan, the captain of a fictional 19th century peasants' team which defeats the British in a thrilling cricket match.
6 *Chak De! India*	f Akshay Kumar stars in this film based on the national hockey team's gold medal-winning campaign in the 1948 London Olympics.
7 *Mary Kom*	g This 2012 biopic starring Irrfan Khan chronicles the life of a soldier-athlete and National Games awardee, who later rebels against the system and becomes a dacoit.
8 *Bhaag Milkha Bhaag*	h Shah Rukh Khan plays a hockey coach to the Indian national women's hockey team.

Whiz fact

King Richard was a 2021 biopic about Richard Williams, coach and father of tennis superstars Serena and Venus Williams. It was nominated for six Academy awards and Will Smith playing the titular role won it for Best Actor in a Leading Role.

Saina, *Azhar* and *Sachin: A Billion Dreams* are some of the biopic films based on the lives and achievements of three living sportspersons who have inspired thousands of young Indians to take up sport.

India Focus

10 A Visit to Central India

Madhya Pradesh was the largest state of India before Chhattisgarh was carved out of it. Now, it is the second-largest state after Rajasthan.

Fill in the blanks with the correct answers from the help box.

1 The town of .... in Madhya Pradesh is known for its Kumbh Mela.

2 .... is the capital city of Chhattisgarh. It is also called Atal Nagar.

3 .... in Madhya Pradesh is famous for its group of Hindu and Jain temples. Its name is derived from the Sanskrit word for 'date palm'.

4 The city of .... in Chhattisgarh gets its name from the Hindi word for 'luxury'. It is famous for its soft colourful Kosa silk saris.

5 The river .... is called the lifeline of Madhya Pradesh. It is one of only three major Indian rivers that flow from east to west.

6 .... in Chhattisgarh is famous for its steel plant.

7 The airport named after Ahilyabai Holkar, the only woman other than Indira Gandhi after whom an Indian airport is named, is located in

....

8 These tribal community ruled between 13th century CE and 19th century CE in an area which is now situated in eastern Madhya Pradesh and western Odisha. Its name is also associated with the southern part of the supercontinent Pangaea. These tribal people are renowned for their art. ....

Help box

Khajuraho | Naya Raipur | Bilaspur | Ujjain | Narmada | Bhilai | Gond | Indore

Whiz quiz

In which state in Central India are these famous sites located?

1 Chitrakoot Falls: ....

2 Jai Vilas Mahal: ....

3 Bhimbetka rock shelters: ....

4 Bhoramdeo Temple: ....

Whiz fact

In British India, a province called Central Provinces was made up of parts of present-day Madhya Pradesh, Chhattisgarh and Maharashtra. Its capital was Nagpur.

15 LIFE ON LAND

Life on Land

11 Friends of the Earth

Environmentalists and conservationists have contributed greatly to creating awareness and preserving the world's environment.

Fill in the blanks with words from the help box to find fascinating facts about some famous conservationists.

1 Rachel Carson was an American marine biologist and conservationist whose book *Silent Spring* created worldwide awareness on the dangers of pesticides. It led to a ban on using .... in the United States.

2 Sundarlal Bahuguna co-founded the non-violent forest conservation campaign known as the .... Movement. For years, he fought for the conservation of the Himalayas.

3 Steve Irwin was an Australian wildlife expert, TV personality and conservationist better known as the .... Hunter.

4 Scottish-American John Muir was a naturalist and author whose activism helped preserve the Yosemite Valley, ... National Park and other wilderness areas in the USA.

5 Wangari Maathai is the Kenyan environmentalist who started the Green Belt Movement and was awarded the Nobel .... Prize for her contribution to sustainable development, democracy and peace.

6 Magsaysay Award-winning water conservationist Rajendra Singh is known as the Rain Man of .... He is credited with getting water to flow again in all five major rivers in the state of Rajasthan.

7 English primatologist Jane Goodall is the world's foremost expert on .... and is the founder of the Roots and Shoots programme.

8 Filmmaker Mike Pandey's documentary *Shores of Silence:* .... *Sharks in India* led to the ban on the killing of these sharks on Indian shores.

9 Brazilian Chico Mendes campaigned for safeguarding the .... rainforest and fought for the human rights of indigenous people.

Help box

Crocodile | DDT | Sequoia | Amazon | Chipko | India | Peace | *Whale* | chimpanzees

Whiz quiz

Name the conservationist who has been credited with being responsible for the creation of the Dudhwa National Park. ....

He is best known for reintroducing which animals into the wild? ....

Whiz fact

Since September 2022, Kuno National Park in Madhya Pradesh saw the entry of 8 cheetahs, 5 female and 3 male, in an effort to reintroduce cheetahs in India after the death of the last of them in the 1950s. They arrived from Namibia. Although a few of them died, some thrived, and have even birthed cubs. Following the birth of 4 new cubs in March 2024, and despite the death of a five-month-old cub and more recently, a male called Pawan, the project is reasonably successful, raising hopes that the cheetah population in the country could be sustained.

Art and Entertainment

12 Art Movements Down the Ages

Each definition of an important world art movement is accompanied by an image illustrating it. Look at the images and choose the correct options.

1 Mannerism is a 16th century art movement that originated in Italy. It is characterised by stylised and elongated/rounded human figures and the use of greys/vivid colours.

2 Impressionism is a 19th century art movement that started in France. It concentrates on depicting the visual impression of a moment with an emphasis on the stark contrast/natural shifting of colours and light. Claude Monet was a pioneer of this movement.

3 Pointillism is a late 19th century painting style where an image is created from dots/dashes of pure colours that blend in at a distance to form recognisable forms and shapes/give a new meaning to strange forms and shapes.

4 Expressionism is an art movement that is aimed at expressing the artist's feelings and experiences rather than depicting the objective reality/beauty of nature.

5 Cubism is an artistic style that aimed at representing natural forms through geometric figures/strange shapes. Cubist painters analyse the subject and break it up into a geometric abstract form.

6 Surrealism is a 20th century art movement that aimed at escaping the idea of reasoning and instead, represented an artist's subconscious mind through precise/strange imagery.

7 Abstract Expressionism is an American art movement that combined abstract forms with planned/spontaneity of artistic expression. Jackson Pollock's technique of splattering paint/adding thick layers of paint onto a canvas laid on the floor is one of the pioneering steps of this movement.

8 Pop Art is an art movement that began in the 1950s in the UK and the USA. It is known for incorporating elements from classical themes/modern pop culture, consumerism and mass media.

Whiz fact

The Bauhaus, also called the International Style, was an art school in Germany which encouraged students to practise not just the visual arts but craft and interior design, architecture, industrial design and typography.

STEM

13 Units of Measurement

Many units of measurement have been named after famous scientists.

Match the scientists and SI units in Column A with what it measures in Column B.

Column A

1 French physicist and mathematician André-Marie Ampère laid down the basis of electromagnetism.

2 Isaac Newton formulated the laws of motion.

3 German physicist Heinrich Hertz proved the existence of electromagnetic waves.

4 French physicist and Nobel laureate, Henri Becquerel was the first person to discover radioactivity.

5 French mathematician, physicist and philosopher Blaise Pascal made important contributions to the study of fluids and vacuum.

Column B

a Frequency

b Radioactivity

c Pressure

d Electrical current

e Force

6 German physicist and mathematician Georg Ohm's work greatly influenced the theory and applications of current electricity.

7 German electrical engineer Werner von Siemens founded the electrical and telecommunications company, Siemens.

8 Volt is named after Italian chemist and physicist Alessandro Volta, who is also credited with inventing the first electrical battery.

9 William Thomson, a famous British mathematical physicist, was given the title Lord Kelvin.

f Electrical conductance

g Thermodynamic temperature

h Electrical resistance

i Electric potential

Whiz quiz

There are seven basic SI units and many derived ones. If kelvin and ampere are two of them, which are the remaining five?

(Hint: These five SI units are not named after scientists.)

....

....

Whiz fact

The International System of Units is abbreviated as SI units from *Système International*, the French version of the name.

14 Startups Around Us

Learning Skills

In the last 20 years or so, new companies, popularly known as startups, have used technology to change the way we live, travel, eat and shop.

Use the fun clues to get the names of 11 such brands and solve the crossword below.

Across

4 India's largest online job portal's name comes straight from a Hindi word. (6)

7 'Make' the most of a holiday, plan a 'trip' with this app! (4, 2, 4)

9 It can be described as India's largest taxi company. (3)

10 To book a hotel room, try this popular startup with a short name. (3)

11 '.. karo' is the tagline of India's largest e-payment brand. (5)

Down

1. An online portal where you can make deals in a snap! (4, 4)
2. This start-up allows you to have a virtual shopping 'kart'! (4, 4)
3. Whether .... or small, never put your eggs in one .... ! (3, 6)
5. According to Amitabh Bachchan, if you have this app, you need no other apps! (4, 4)
6. This is a portal you would use if you were hungry! (6)
8. This site is useful for making a 'journey'. (5)

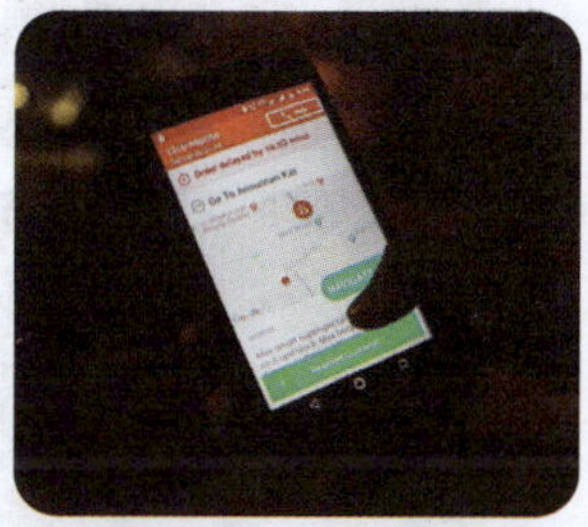

Whiz fact

A startup company that is valued at US $1 billion is termed a unicorn. Of the startups featured in this crossword, the answer to 2 Down was acquired by Walmart for a whopping US $17 billion. Write its name here. ....

Whiz quiz

Identify these two startup entities from the world of education.

1. An educational organisation based in Mountain View, California, that sets up online tools to help educate students in science and mathematics, and also helps prepare them for college entrance tests ....
2. Bhavish Aggarwal is a serial entrepreneur associated with many startup unicorns. In 2024, which company entered the Unicorn Club as a "large language model artificial intelligence company", making it India's first AI startup to become a unicorn?..

World Around Us

15 Royal Heads

Monarchies are countries ruled by kings or queens. Once upon a time, these were very common, but today only 43 nations have a monarch as the Head of State.

Identify these monarchs by writing the correct number in the boxes.

1 

2 

3 

4 

5 

6 

a Emperor Naruhito of Japan 

b King Maha Vajiralongkorn Bodindradebayavarangkun of Thailand 

c Emir Sheikh Tamim Bin Hamad Al-Thani of Qatar 

d Druk Gyalpo Jigme Khesar Namgyel Wangchuck of Bhutan 

e King Frederik X of Denmark 

f King Mswati III of Eswatini 

Whiz fact

French soldier Jean Bernadotte became the King of Sweden with Napoleon Bonaparte's support. However, he was so popular that the Bernadotte family still rules in Sweden today, even after over 200 years!

16 Sanchi Stupa

Right in the heart of India lies an extraordinary complex of Buddhist art, sculpture and architecture, a UNESCO World Heritage Site—the Sanchi Stupa.

Read these paragraphs about this site and fill in the blanks using the help box. But watch out! There are some extra incorrect answers in the help box.

1 The Sanchi Stupa is a Buddhist Complex whose construction began in ancient times, in the .... BCE, under the great Emperor Ashoka.

2 Sanchi is in modern ...., not far from Bhopal. On the way, we would cross 23½° N or the Tropic of Cancer, called .... in Hindi.

3 The complex saw a lot of construction for about a thousand years, until the decline of .... in India, towards the 19th century. In 1818–1819, the complex was rediscovered by General Henry Taylor, a .... officer. Another century later, under John Marshall, restoration work was carried out.

4 Various episodes from the life of Buddha were sculpted, as were depictions of the sacred .... tree and other Buddhist symbols, like lions and ...., scenes from the life of Ashoka and other kings, deities and devotees from around the world.

Help box

British	Hinduism	3rd century	Buddhism	lotuses
Devi	French	Madhya Pradesh	Bodhi	*Kark Rekha*

Whiz quiz

The Sanchi Stupa features on one of the new currency notes issued by the Government of India. Which one is it? Write it here. ....

STEM

17 Great Mathematicians

Mathematics may not be everyone's favourite subject, but what would humankind be without it? Geniuses, since ancient times have tried to count, calculate and codify the world of numbers to help us make sense of the universe.

Read the clues and solve this acrostic. If your answers are correct, the column will contain a crucial branch of mathematics. Each clue has extra rebus clues to help you get (and spell) the answer.

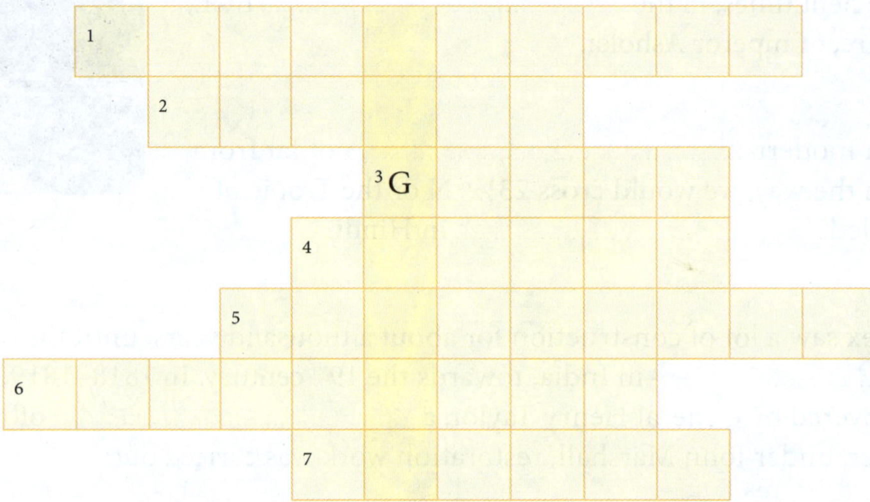

1 A Greek whose most famous theorem concerns right-angled triangles

 – ON+ A +  +  – G – S ....

2 A Greek who lived in Alexandria (Egypt), whose work titled *Elements* is the main source of ancient geometry

Anagram of CUE + 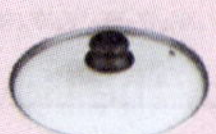 ....

3 This German child prodigy was known for his work on algebra, astronomy and map-making.

Indian music equivalent of MI in the musical scale + plural of ME + S

....

4 A well-known English physicist who independently invented calculus to prove his laws of motion

Opposite of OLD + synonym of 1000 KILOGRAMS

....

5 An Italian who described a sequence which begins with 1, 1, 2, 3, 5, 8, 13, 21, 34, 55, ...

Synonym of LIE + opposite of OFF + ACCIDENT – DENT ....

6 A Frenchman who bridged the gap between algebra and geometry, laying the foundations of modern geometry

 – K +  + 

– C ....

7 A French prodigy whose correspondence with Pierre de Fermat led to the creation of the probability theory

P + RASCAL – R ....

Whiz fact

Algebra is the study of mathematical symbols and the rules for 'playing' with them. The term comes from the Arabic phrase *al-jabr,* which means 'reunion of broken parts', taken from a book *Ilm al-jabr wa'l-mubala* written by the Persian mathematician and astronomer al-Khwarizmi.

18 Self-Defence in Animals

Every living being in nature has evolved defence mechanisms to protect itself from predators.

Match the animal with the defence mechanism it uses by writing the correct letter in the boxes.

1 

Bee

2 

Octopus

3 

Opossum

4 

Owl butterfly

5 

Ladybird

6 

Hagfish

a Displays a pattern of large eyes on its wing surface to scare the attacker

b Lies still as if it is dead, in the presence of predators

c This colourful insect secretes a foul-tasting liquid when threatened

d Stings the enemy if it feels threatened

e Oozes suffocating slime from its elongated body that envelops the predator in a fatal mass of fibrous goo

f Squirts a cloud of ink at its predator from its tentacles

7 

Lizard

9 

Porcupine

11 

Snail

g Releases poison through its skin to kill predators like snakes and spiders

h Hides in the shell on its back at the slightest threat

i Loses the end of its tail, allowing it to escape when threatened

j Expands its neck collar, opens its mouth and waves its tail to scare away predators

k When threatened, it coils and lets its quills bristle and protrude outwards

l This black and white animal sprays a musk causing temporary blindness to the victim

8 

Skunk

10 

Poison dart frog

12 

Australian frilled lizard

Whiz fact

The electric eel can discharge up to 600 volts to stun or even kill its prey.

World Around Us

19 Italy, Here We Come!

From culture to cuisine, from history to fashion, from art to cinema, Italy makes us say, *'Che bello!'* (How lovely!)

Pick the option with an Italian connect in each of these sentences.

1 The Carpathians/Apennines are a mountain range that run from North to South down the spine of Italy.

2 Garibaldi/Otto von Bismarck is hailed as the father of the unification of Italy.

3 Latin/Sanskrit is the mother language from which Italian language is derived.

4 The arena in ancient Rome where gladiator games were held is called the Colosseum/La Maestranza.

5 Sicily/Sardinia is the largest island in the Mediterranean Sea.

6 José Saramago/Dante is the father of Italian literature, a poet who wrote the *Divine Comedy*.

7 Bugatti/Maserati is a well-known Italian sports car manufacturer.

8 The five seas that hug the coast of Italy are the Mediterranean, Adriatic, Tyrrhenian, Ligurian and Aegean/Ionian.

9 Yodelling/Opera is a stage drama set to music that includes performances by trained singers.

10 People fleeing from the armies of Attila the Hun established Vicenza/Venice on some islands in the Adriatic Sea.

Whiz fact

The colour magenta gets its name from the Battle of Magenta, which took place near the town of Magenta, situated close to Milan.

20 Forts of India

Fill in the blanks with the correct names of these forts. To further help you find the answers, the first letters have been provided.

1 Home to Rani Lakshmi Bai, the J .... Fort in Uttar Pradesh is over 400 years old and flaunts the Bundela and Maratha styles of architecture.

2 The G .... Fort in Madhya Pradesh is one of the largest forts in India. It exhibits rare artefacts dating back to the 1st and 2nd centuries BCE.

3 The J .... Fort in Rajasthan is also known as Sonar Quila because of the beige colour of the fort, which complements the sandy Thar Desert. It was built in 1156 CE and was used as a refuge for travellers on the Silk Route until the British Raj.

4 The name of the G .... Fort built on a granite hill means 'round shaped hill'. Located near present-day Hyderabad, it was first built by the Kakatiya dynasty.

5 The B .... Fort in Karnataka has the striking monument called the '*Gol Gumbaz*', a huge mausoleum which is the second-largest domed top in the world after St. Peter's Basilica in Rome.

6 The R .... Fort served as the first capital of Shivaji's kingdom and stands on the Sahyadri mountain range in Maharashtra. It was impregnable, which was why the British called it the 'Gibraltar of the East'.

Whiz fact

According to the *Arthashastra*, based on their type of defence, there are 6 types of forts—Jaladurg (water fort), Marudurg (desert fort), Giridurg (hill fort), Vanadurg (forest fort), Mahidurg (earthen fort) and Naridurg (human fort).

21 Eponyms

An eponym is a word used for a product, invention or scientific discovery that is named after the person most closely associated with it.

Fill in the blanks with the words from the help box to learn about them.

1. American Civil War general Ambrose .... lent a version of his name to the hair grown down the side of a man's face, because he sported this style.
2. Arthur Wellesley, first Duke of ...., popularised this loose waterproof rubber boot to be worn in wet or muddy conditions.

3. The Scottish inventor of a waterproof raincoat made of rubberised fabric, Charles .... gave his name to this item of clothing.
4. Candido Enzo ...., an Italian immigrant to the United States invented the whirlpool bath of the same name for his son, who was born with rheumatoid arthritis.

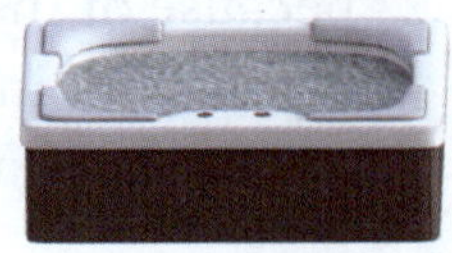

5. British Major General Henry .... perfected a hollow cannonball filled with lead shot that burst in mid-air, a word still synonymous with fragmentation from artillery shells.

6. James Brudenell, the seventh Earl of ...., was an army Major General who gave his name to the knitted garment that has buttons down the front, distinguishing it from the pullover.
7. 19th century French acrobat Jules .... wore a skin-tight top leaving the legs free. Today, this garment is worn by ballet dancers, gymnasts and circus performers.

8. This popular food was created in the 18th century when John Montagu, the fourth Earl of .... wanted to be served meat placed between two slices of bread so he could keep playing cards even as he ate.

Help box

Mackintosh	Leotard	Shrapnel	Cardigan
Jacuzzi	Wellington	Burnside	Sandwich

Whiz fact

Jumbo was a famous circus elephant whose name popularised the use of the word 'jumbo' as a synonym for 'huge'.

22 Safety in the Cyber World

Life Skills

The Internet is a great place to know more about things we don't know and to keep in touch with our friends and family. But it also has dangers and threats that we should know about.

Match the clues in Column A with those in Column B to show that you know how to be safe online.

Column A	Column B
1 Sites that have HTTPS in the address bar	a log out of all websites you've accessed and close all the windows you've opened before leaving the computer.
2 When working on a public computer, always	b are safer than sites that have HTTP.
3 Never share your passwords	c without scanning it using an antivirus program.
4 Even if a bank employee calls or emails you,	d unless you have the copyright to do so.
5 Unless you are thirteen years or older,	e do not share your login details with them.
6 Do not download and share music and movies on the Internet	f with anyone.
7 Never open a file on someone else's USB or a file downloaded from the Internet	g do not sign up for sites like Facebook, YouTube and Instagram.

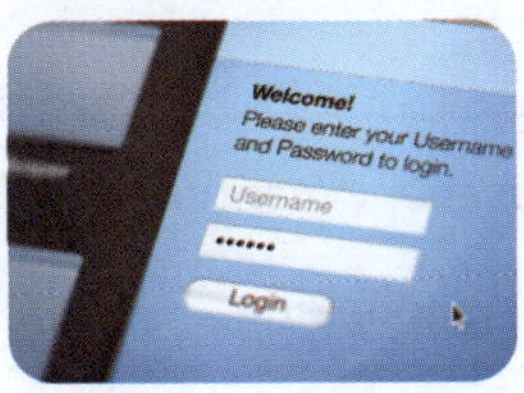

Whiz fact

A US programmer named Ray Tomlinson developed the email system and sent the first ever email in 1971.

Life on Land

23 Plastic

In any 'Save Earth' discussion, one of the biggest villains is plastic. Plastic has been around for a little more than a century, and modern living is impossible without it. But everyone knows that it is bad for our environment.

Read the text and complete the story of plastic with words from the help box. Watch out, as there are 12 blanks and 16 answers!

1. Plastic mostly comes from petroleum or natural gas, which are both .... The word plastic comes from the Greek word *plastikos* means 'that which can be .... or moulded'.

2. In fact, apart from being flexible, plastic is ...., durable and cheap to produce, which is why it is so popular.
3. The first synthetically produced plastic was called bakelite by a Belgian-American chemist, ... in 1907. Plastic then slowly began to replace other materials, like metals, leather, natural cloth, glass and paper over the next few .... By the 1970s, scientists realised that plastic had become a menace.

4. Plastic items like bags, plates and spoons, straws, and bottles go into .... and often end up in the .... .They form huge floating islands of plastic rubbish called marine garbage patches. Since plastic does not .... easily, these plastic islands will never ever vanish in our lifetimes!
5. Then there are .... that wash out from sinks and basins, washing machines, factories and thrown-away clothes, that birds and fish ...., causing them to starve, fall ill, choke and die very painful deaths.

6. Inventors have been busy trying to come up with alternatives to plastic. A small amount of plastic is now being made from .... sources, such as cellulose and starch. Called ...., it could become an important alternative in the future.

Help box

Leo Baekeland | lightweight | microplastics | shaped | plant-based | centuries | fossil fuels | swallow | broken | river | ocean | decades | heavy | biodegrade | landfills | bioplastic

Whiz fact

Plastic bags take up to 20 years to decompose, while other plastic things, like straws, diapers, bottles and toothbrushes can take hundreds of years to decompose. We might not be able to completely get rid of toothbrushes, but we can certainly make efforts to reduce our use of plastic straws, cups and bottles, can't we?

India Focus

24 What's in a Train Name?

Use the clues and help box to fill in the terminus of each train mentioned below.

1. The Black Diamond Express connects coal-mining cities in East-Central India. It runs from Howrah to ....

2. *Thirukkural* was written by Thiruvalluvar, whose statue is found at the southern tip of the Indian subcontinent. The Thirukkural Express runs from Hazrat Nizamuddin to ....

3. *Maitree* means 'friendship'. The Maitree Express is the first passenger railway link between Bangladesh and India since 1965, when it was shut down. It links Kolkata to ....

4. The Ashram Express is named after a famous ashram on the banks of the River Sabarmati and runs from Delhi to ....

5. The Gitanjali Express, named after Rabindranath Tagore's collection of poems, runs from Mumbai to ....

6. The *Akal Takht* means the 'throne of the timeless one' and is one of the five Sikh *takhts*. Named after it, The Akal Takht Express connects Kolkata to ....

7. Konark, a small town in Odisha, is famous for its Sun Temple. The Konark Express connects Mumbai to ....

8. Tipu Sultan was known as the Tiger of Mysuru, but was finally defeated by the English. The Tippu Express runs from Bangalore to ....

Help box

Amritsar | Ahmedabad | Bhubaneswar | Dhaka | Dhanbad | Howrah | Kanyakumari | Mysore

Whiz fact

The Vande Bharat Express (also known as Train 18) has been designed and built by the Integral Coach Factory (ICF) in Chennai and is one of the first semi-high-speed trains to be built in India.

World Today

25 Design Thinking

Design thinking is a methodology that focuses on solving problems using innovation and a solution-oriented approach. Companies, products, and services increasingly use it.

Five Steps of design thinking

Empathy	Definition	Ideation:	Prototyping	Testing
Why: To understand user needs, desires and challenges	**Why:** To Identify user patterns and refine the problem scope.	**Why:** To generate solution-oriented ideas	**Why:** To test the effectiveness of solutions.	**Why:** To assess solution effectiveness.
Action: Observe and collect data about users without biases.	**Action:** Analyze the collected data and formulate a precise problem statement.	**Action:** Brainstorm and develop creative solution to address pain points.	**Action:** Create prototypes to bring ideas to life and allow users to interact with them.	**Action:** Gather feedback to improve the solution and address the problem.

Some companies have used design thinking very effectively. Below are statements about three such companies. The statements may be 'problem statements' or 'solution statements'.

Statements

1. Children do not like to brush their teeth.
2. Sports footwear should aid, not hinder, the performance of the sportsperson.
3. Viewers spend too much time and effort while trying to watch a program or film.
4. The introduction of short trailer videos and the Shuffle button customized viewer preferences and improved user experience.
5. The design team used bright colours and engaging graphics to make children look forward to brushing their teeth.
6. Customers have a wide choice of footwear, since most shoes are the same.
7. Too many options can confuse viewers with too much choice, and decision-making is a chore.
8. The brand added transparent panels that showcased wearers' socks, which was a fun and funky element.
9. Children use their palms rather than their fingers to grip toothbrushes.

10 The company introduced options such as "Skip Intro" and "Because you watched", to reduce effort.

11 The company introduced pressurised air technology, which enhanced athletic performance.

12 The company introduced 'squish gripper' brushes with wider and softer handles.

For each company shown below, indicate which statements are connected to that company. One has been done for you.

t	Company 1 Oral B	Company 2 Netflix	Company 3 Nike
Problem Statement 1	9. Children use their palms rather than their fingers to grip toothbrushes.		
Solution Statement 1			
Problem Statement 2			
Solution Statement 2			

Whiz activity

Do you know of any company, brand or product that introduced innovation or design to improve customer experience and was a huge success? Write about it here.

....

....

....

....

Literacy Skills

26 Technology of the Future

Technology is changing so fast that if someone had gone to sleep in 2000 and woke up in 2021, they would not recognise the world in which they woke up.

TECHNOLOGY

Pick the correct word from the help box to complete these facts about the technology of the future.

1 Universal translators will be able to translate something like 6,000 .... into your native language. Imagine the number of books, movies and conversations you could enjoy!

2 Harry Potter made the idea of the .... popular. People are looking forward to reducing both travel time and the number of road accidents by using this.

3 The Internet of Things (IoT) is a concept in which all appliances and devices will be connected to the Internet. This will help them .... with each other without our having to turn them on or off. For instance, the toaster would switch itself on after you finish your bath so that your breakfast is ready by the time you get dressed.

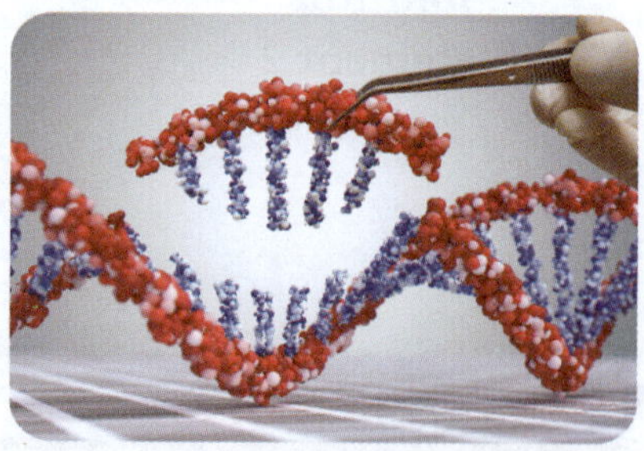

4 Geome editing involves altering .... to improve human life. It may result in humans being born without diseases and may even create 'super humans' who don't get tired, don't need sleep, etc.

5 Ingestible robots are robots that can be sent into the bloodstream to repair the body from inside so that expensive .... can be minimised or avoided.

6 Scientists are trying to .... Mars as an alternative place for our increasing population. With climate change, it may become essential for us to find another home to live in.

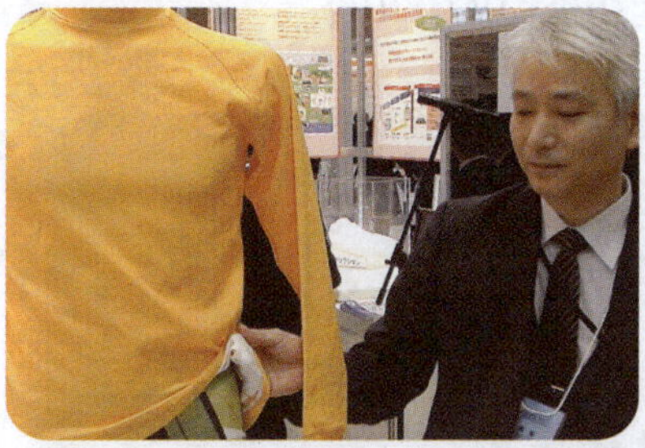

7 Nanotech fibres with smart technology will create smart clothes that help the wearer to always be comfortable. The technology will regulate .... and possibly change shape to fit the wearer.

8 The Singularity is the concept that humans and machines will one day become one, with all human .... sharing the same space as machines.

Help box

communicate	DNA	surgeries	minds
body temperature	flying car	colonise	languages

Whiz quiz

Which of these technology buzzwords have become realities?

1 Facial recognition ☐ 2 Solar power ☐

3 Super-speed trains ☐ 4 Heart monitoring clothes ☐

Whiz fact

In May 2022, Google Translate Services added eight new Indian languages, including Sanskrit, Assamese, Bhojpuri, Dogri, Konkani, Maithili, Mizo and Meitei (Manipuri) and in 2024, 7 Indian regional dialects such as Awadhi, Bodo, Khasi, Kokborok, Marwadi, Santali, and Tulu were added. Machine learning is making serious inroads into human lives!

27 Touring India

India is a land of diversity. You can visit a jungle, the mountains, the sea or a historic place, depending on what activities you feel like doing.

Look at these pictures and write the locations where you can pursue these activities.

1 

Snorkelling in ....

2 

Cruise through .... in a houseboat

3 

Visit the Hawa Mahal in ....

4 

Rhino-spotting in ....

5 

Skiing in ....

6 

Bird watching at the ....

7

Visit the Rani ki vav in ....

8

Paragliding in..

9

Relaxing on a beach in ....

10

Tiger-spotting in..

11

Visit the Gol Gumbaz in ....

12

River rafting in ....

Help box

Bandhavgarh National Park	Kerala	Jaipur	Baliman Dara
Keoladeo National Park	Kaziranga National Park	Rishikesh	Gulmarg
Patan	Port Blair	Bijapur	Goa

Whiz fact

The Vivek Express runs from Dibrugarh in Assam to Kanyakumari in Tamil Nadu, taking over 80 hours to cover 4,262 km, whilst halting at over 50 stations. One can travel across most of India and enjoy varied sceneries on this train.

28 Institutions of Higher Learning

Students long for the time when they can go to university and study the subjects of their choice and train to specialise in fields that interest them.

Use the clues and the help box to correctly identify the names of various universities in India and abroad, and then fill in the blanks.

1. Filmmaker Satyajit Ray and economist Amartya Sen studied at this university in West Bengal. It has the Hindi word for 'world' in its name. ....

2. The alumni of this university in California includes founders of Google, Yahoo, Hewlett-Packard and Nike. It has the brand name of a car in its name. ....

3. Dating back to 1096, it is the oldest university in the English speaking world. It has the name of an animal in it. ....

4. Once known as King's College, this university is in New York City. Its name sounds similar to the name of a country and is the exact name of a district in USA. ....

5. Founded in 1701, this US university is named after a governor of the English East India Company. The name rhymes with pale! ....

6 This university was founded by Ezra and Andrew D White in 1865 at Ithaca. It has the name of a food in its name. ....

7 The oldest university in the USA, its motto is 'Veritas' or 'Truth'. It includes a word that denotes laughter.

....

8 The leading university in Nepal is named after a King of Nepal. Its name includes a synonym for the word 'three'. ....

9 Named after an ancient university, this was started in 2014 with Amartya Sen as its Chancellor. Its name has a common joining word in it. ....

10 Started in 1209, it is the second oldest university in England and counts Isaac Newton as one of its alumni. Its name includes the name of a structure used to cross a river. ....

Help box

- Harvard University
- Stanford University
- Tribhuvan University
- Cambridge University
- Columbia University
- Oxford University
- Yale University
- Nalanda University
- Visva-Bharati University
- Cornell University

Whiz fact

There is a bell in the Oxford University library that hasn't stopped ringing for more than 175 years. Researchers are afraid that opening the bell would ruin the experiment to see how long it will last.

29 Autobiographies

An autobiography is the story of a person's life written by that person.

Match these personalities to their autobiographies.

Personality

1 

Nelson Mandela

2 

Dr. A.P.J. Abdul Kalam

3 

Mahatma Gandhi

4 

Abhinav Bindra

Autobiography

a *A Shot at History* was written by India's first Olympic gold medallist.

b *Long Walk to Freedom* was written by a leader who fought against apartheid in his country.

c *Wings of Fire* was written by a scientist who became the President of India.

d *The Story of My Experiments with Truth* was written by a famous person who was lovingly called Bapu.

5

Maya Angelou

6

Michael Jackson

7

Helen Keller

8

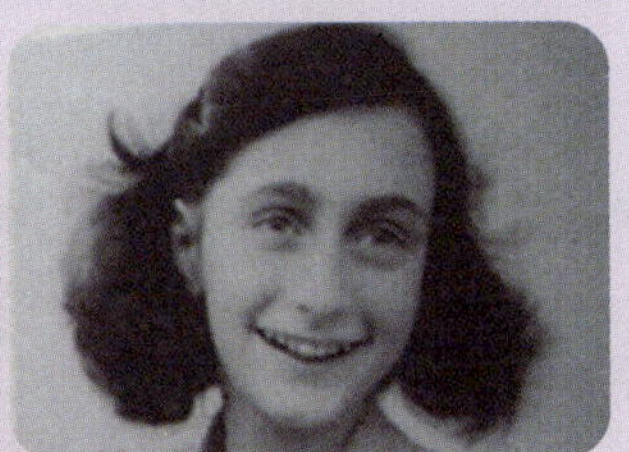

Anne Frank

e *The Diary of a Young Girl* was written by a young victim of the Holocaust.

f *The Story of My Life* was written by the first deaf-blind person to earn a Bachelor of Arts degree.

g *Moonwalk* was written by a famous singer and composer famous for his dance moves.

h *I Know Why the Caged Bird Sings* was written by an American poet, singer and civil rights activist.

Whiz quiz

Who wrote these autobiographies?

1. *Dreams From My Father* ....
2. *Toward Freedom* ....
3. *The Race of My Life* ....

Whiz fact

Man's Search for Meaning by Viktor Frankl is the story of Frankl's survival in Auschwitz and other concentration camps in Germany during World War II.

World Around Us

30 Intangible Heritage

Some aspects of culture like song, music, drama, cuisine and festivals are called intangible heritage because these have to be experienced and performed. UNESCO aims to spread awareness of these and safeguard them.

Use the help box, the image and the clues provided to identify the intangible heritage and fill in the blanks.

1. In Indonesia, hot wax is poured on fabric to create patterns, after which the waxed fabrics are dyed with vegetable colours. ....

2. In Turkey, this traditional symbol of hospitality, friendship, refinement and entertainment is celebrated in literature and songs as well. ....

3. In Bangladesh, musicians travel from place to place and earn their living by singing to the accompaniment of simple instruments. ....

4. Originally from Africa, this Brazilian practice performed by men is fight, dance, sport, art form and tradition, all rolled into one. ....

5. Andalusia in Spain is the heartland of this artistic expression fusing song, dance and musicianship.
....

6 In India, a tribe that catches snakes and trades in snake venom wears black costumes and performs a dance resembling the movement of serpents. ....

7 In Cambodia, this form of Khmer shadow theatre is considered sacred and features two metre high puppets made of leather.

....

8 In Italy, experts of soil, weather conditions and local geography take their trained dogs to sniff out this delicacy from beneath the ground to use in cooking. ....

9 In Argentina and Uruguay, this ballroom dance is characterised by marked rhythms and postures and abrupt pauses. ....

10 In China, along the Yangtze river, this event includes a memorial ceremony to a local hero and various sporting events such as races and willow shooting.

....

Help box

Bauls | Tango | Sbek Thom | Capoeira | Batik | Kalbelia
Dragon boat festival | Coffee | Flamenco | Truffle hunting

Whiz fact

The traditions and festivities associated with Durga Puja, celebrated with much pomp and splendour especially in Kolkata, and the Garba Dance, a vibrant folk dance of Gujarat and a staple of the nine-night Navaratri festival, have been included in the UNESCO Intangible Cultural Heritage List in 2021 and 2023 respectively.

STEM

31 Space Exploration

For as long as humans have existed, space has played an important part in our lives. Early man navigated paths across land and oceans using the stars.

Use the clues and pictures to solve the crossword relating to the history of space exploration.

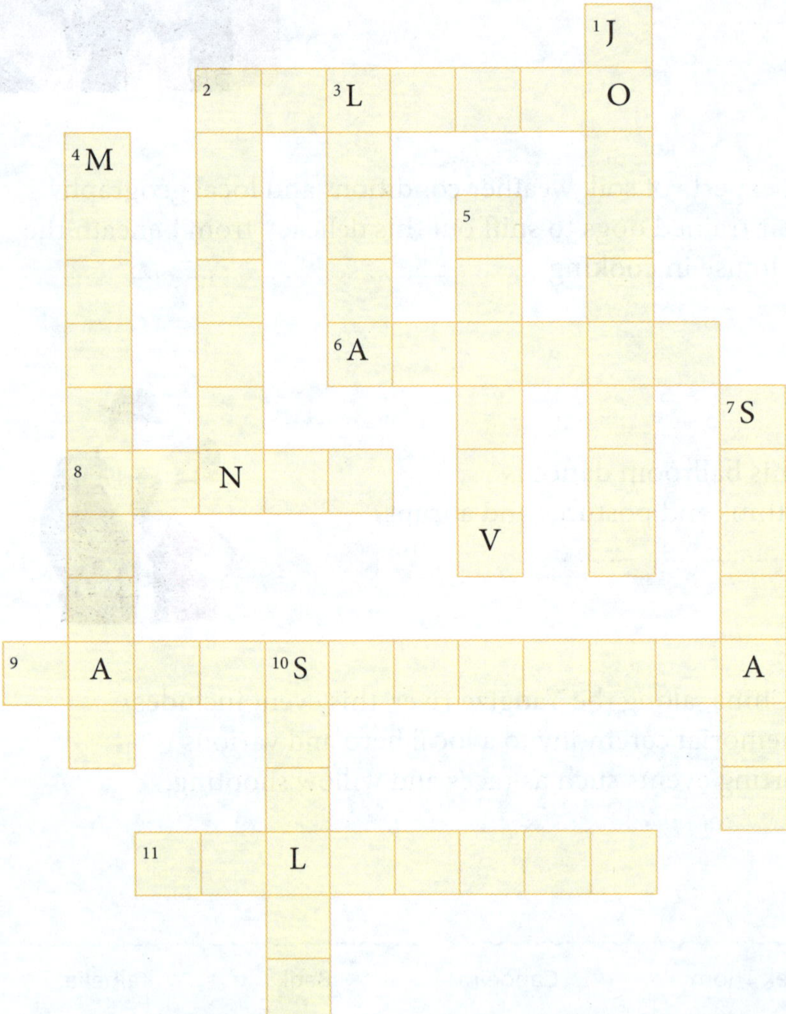

ED Image

Across

2 Which US probe, named after an Italian astronomer, reached Jupiter in 1995 and revealed hitherto unknown information about its moons?

6 What name was given to the series of American space missions in the 1960s and early 1970s that saw successful landings on the surface of the moon?

8 In 1966, which Russian probe was the first to land on the moon?

9 In 1984, who became the first Indian cosmonaut?

11 Which space shuttle, first launched by NASA in 1981, flew twenty-seven successful missions before it met with a disastrous accident killing Kalpana Chawla and six other crew members in 2003?

Down

1 Who was the first American to orbit the Earth?

2 In 1961, which Russian Air Force pilot became the first man to travel into space?

3 What was the name of the stray dog from Moscow who became the first living creature to orbit the Earth in 1957?

4 What is India's Mars Orbiter Mission which was successfully launched in 2014 called?

5 Who was the first person to step out of a spacecraft and walk in space?

7 In 1961, who became the first American to go into space?

10 Which was the first ever American space station which orbited Earth from 1973 to 1979?

Whiz quiz

Find out the answers and fill in the blanks about India's recent space achievement.

India made history when its space agency .... launched .... from the .... at Sriharikota, off the coast of .... on 14 July 2023. It consisted of a lunar lander called .... and a lunar rover called ....

On 5 August, India became the first nation in the world to land on the moon's ....

Whiz fact

According to NASA, it takes astronauts 45 minutes to put on a spacesuit, but it protects them from temperature as low as −157°C to a high temperature of upto 121°C.

Natural World

32 Most Biodiverse Countries

The more climate zones and landforms a country has, the more biodiversity it is likely to have.

Match the two halves of each fact to find out about the biodiversity of many countries.

1 The United States has more	a rainforest in the world and is home to 730 bird species.
2 Colombia has more than 314 different types	b of which are endemic and 612 species of birds.
3 Papua New Guinea has the third largest	c of ecosystems.
4 Brazil has over 55,000 plant species,	d than 17,000 species of plants.
5 The Philippines has over 9,250 plants, one third	e the most known number in any single country.
6 Peru has over 500 species of mammals,	f in Africa. It has 900 species of butterflies.
7 The Democratic Republic of Congo is the source of half of the freshwater	g It also has 1592 bird species.
8 Indonesia has 25,000 flowering plants, of which 55% are endemic.	h of which 70 are endemic.

Whiz quiz

Which of the following areas in India are known as hotspots of biodiversity?

1 Sunderbans

2 Western Ghats

3 Eastern Ghats

4 Gangetic Plain

Whiz fact

India is home to 410 mammal species, of which 41 are endemic to India. Of these 16 are only found in the Western Ghats and 10 only in the Andaman & Nicobar Islands.

33 The Revolutionaries of 1857

India's First War of Independence began in Meerut in May 1857 and was largely suppressed by September 1857, with significant events continuing into early 1858.

Fill in the blanks with the names of these revolutionaries of 1857 using the clues and the help box.

1. A religious leader of Faizabad, ... was known as the 'Lighthouse of the Rebellion' in Awadh. He was killed by treachery for a reward of 50,000 pieces of silver.

2. The king of Jagdishpur in modern-day Bihar, ... was nearly 80-years-old and in failing health when he brought down the Union Jack and flew his own flag from the Jagdishpur Fort, for which the Hindi word for 'brave' is prefixed to his name.

3. .... was an Indian soldier who played a key part in events immediately preceding the Revolt of 1857. He was executed by hanging, shortly before the First War of Independence began.

4. An adopted son of Peshwa Baji Rao II, ... joined the revolt because he was deprived of his pension by the British. He captured Kanpur and proclaimed himself the Peshwa, but his victory was short-lived.

5. A 22-year-old queen, ... led her armies against the British when they refused to accept the claim of her adopted son to the throne of Jhansi. She fought gallantly and succeeded in capturing Gwalior.

6. .... was an ageing Mughal ruler who was declared the Emperor of Hindustan in 1857 by mutinying soldiers. He was captured and deported to Rangoon where he died in 1862.

Help box

Mangal Pandey | Veer Kunwar Singh | Maulvi Ahmadullah Shah | Nana Saheb | Bahadur Shah II | Rani Lakshmibai

Whiz fact

What's in a name? The events of 1857 were variously described as the Indian Mutiny, The Indian Revolt, the Sepoy Revolt, and many such terms. Revolutionary leader-activist Vinayak Damodar Savarkar was the first to formally use the term "War of Independence" in a 1909 book. India's first Prime Minister, Jawaharlal Nehru, officially prefixed the word "First" to indicate that India fought many more wars before finally shaking off the foreign yoke and gaining independence from the British.

Art and Entertainment

34 Decode the music and the musician!

Worldwide, some musicians have achieved phenomenal success for their catchy songs, unique voices, viral videos and riveting personalities.

In this triple-matching task, you will:

A. *Read the descriptions and match them to the correct song and singer.*

B. *Unjumble the anagrams to identify these enormously popular world musicians.*

C. *Use the numbers in brackets next to each word jumble to determine the number of letters in each word of the song title.*

Anagram	Description	Musicians
1 SOOLYVERT (4, 5)	a This track, peaking at number 3 on the Billboard Countdown 200, was released by this once-child actress and Nigerian artiste Rema in 2022.	i LATYRO WIFTS  ....
2 REKIFWOR (8)	b This highly popular 2009 track was rerecorded as the singer's "version" and rereleased in 2021. The performer's 2024 Eras Tour has made history as the highest-grossing concert tour ever.	ii TAKY PREYR  ....
3 DAWNCOLM (4, 4)	c This song accompanied the circus acts in the 2012 animated film *Madagascar 3: Most Wanted in Europe*. This record-breaking singer performed the song at US President Joe Biden's inauguration in 2020.	iii LENESA SOGEM  ....

4 FUMLTEPI (4, 2, 2)

....

5 MAYSENESO (4, 2, 2)

....

6 YEPOOHUFAS (5, 2, 3)

....

d This number from the album 30 won the Grammy for Best Pop Solo Performance in 2023. The UK-born singer is known for her powerful mezzo-soprano voice and albums having numbers for names.

e This 2017 song was from the album ÷ (Divide) by this English singer-songwriter. The song is the second most streamed song on Spotify, with over 3.6 billion streams.

f This 2022 track from the movie *The Black Panther: Wakanda Forever* won this Barbadian singer an Academy Award nomination

iv HANANRI

....

v EDEAL

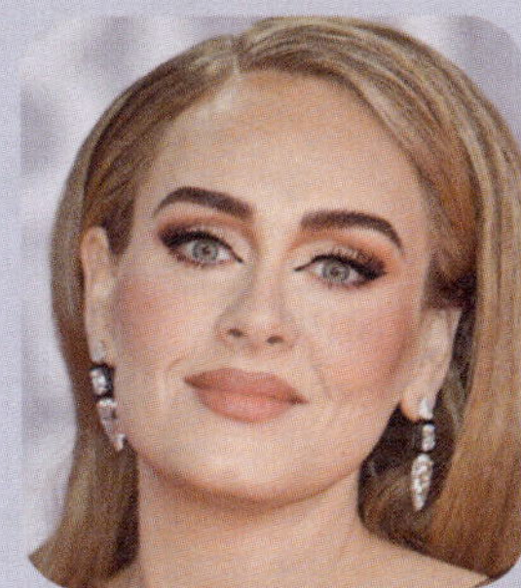

....

vi DE ERASHEN

....

Whiz fact

Originally proposed and developed by musician-composer N Ravikiran and further developed by British-American composer Robert Morris, melharmony is a new form of musical composition, combining the melodic classical music systems of India and western classical music systems, which are based on harmonies. Talk of the best of both worlds!

Whiz quiz

Name the top six bestselling artists of all time, with claimed sales of over 250 million records worldwide.

.................................., ..., ...,

.................................., ..., ...

India Focus

35 Northeast India's Glorious Past

Match the name of each state of Northeast India with a glimpse of its history.

State	Historical Glimpse
1 Assam	a This landlocked state bordering Bangladesh and Myanmar became a Union Territory in 1972 and a state in 1987.
2 Meghalaya	b India's easternmost state, the McMahon line separates this state from the Sino-Tibetan border.
3 Nagaland	c This state existed as a province during British times as well and was once ruled by Ahom Kings.
4 Tripura	d This state was ruled by the kings of the Chogyal dynasty before it joined the Indian Union in 1975.
5 Mizoram	e This state came under British rule in the 1870s; its capital is nicknamed 'Scotland of the East' because of the similarities in landscape.
6 Manipur	f This state was ruled by the Manikya dynasty for hundreds of years and is home to magnificent monuments such as the 19th century Ujjayanta Palace and medieval rock-cut carvings.
7 Sikkim	g Its capital was the scene of the Battle of Kohima during the World War II, in which British and Indian troops fought and won against Japanese forces.
8 Arunachal Pradesh	h A state in 1972, the game of polo was introduced to Europeans in this state.

Whiz fact

Nagaland, Meghalaya, Arunachal Pradesh and Mizoram were all carved out of Assam from 1963 onwards.

STEM

36 Extremes of the Universe

The universe has no centre. It is expanding all the time, so it is impossible to reach its edge. Despite this, there are many extremes in the universe.

Match the columns to find out about the extremes of the universe.

Extreme	Clue
1 The Boomerang Nebula is located in the Centaurus constellation. It is the coldest object in the universe.	a It was launched into space in 1977 and left our solar system in 2013.
2 The highest mountain known is on the asteroid Vesta.	b It was 5.5 trillion degree Celsius, 3,60,000 times hotter than the temperature at the Sun's core.
3 The farthest star humans have ever seen is the star called Earendel.	c Ganymede is one of the 79 known moons of Jupiter.
4 The hottest man-made temperature was created by physicists trying to recreate the conditions immediately after the Big Bang.	d It took 12.9 billion years for its light to reach Earth.
5 The largest known star is UY Scuti, located in the Scutum constellation in the Milky Way galaxy.	e It is about 22 km in height, making it almost three times taller than Mount Everest.
6 The man-made object farthest from Earth is the spacecraft Voyager 1.	f It is 30 times the mass of our Sun.
7 The largest moon in our solar system orbits Jupiter. It is also the only moon with its own magnetic field.	g Its temperature is –272° Celsius.

Whiz fact

If you were travelling at the speed of light, you would go around the Earth 7½ times in one second!

37 GI Tagged Products of India

A Geographical Indication (GI) is a sign used on products that have a specific geographical origin and possess qualities or a reputation that are due to that origin. To function as a GI, a sign must identify a product as originating in a given place.

Using the state maps and the help box as clues, identify some GI tagged products and fill in the blanks with the name of the states of India that these products are from.

1  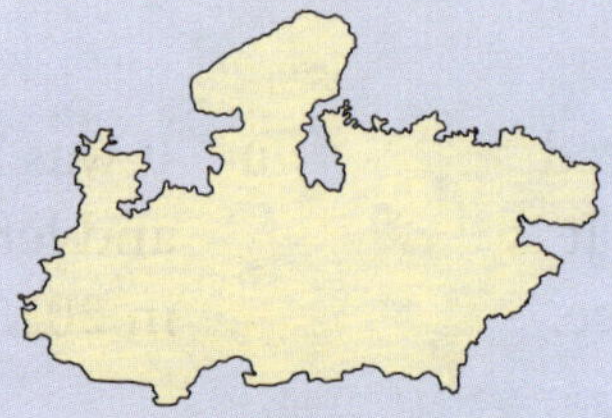

Chanderi fabric of ....

2  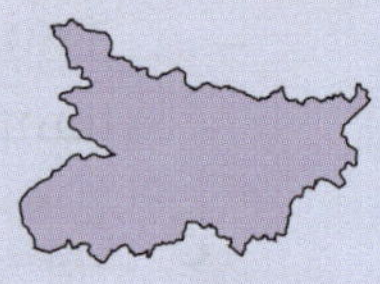

Madhubani paintings of ....

3  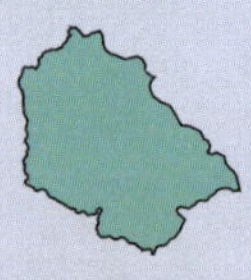

Kani shawls of ....

4  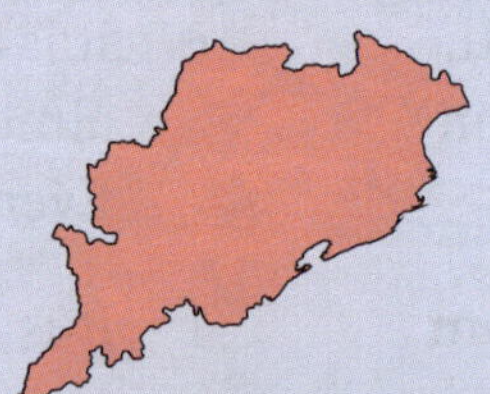

Pattachitra of ....

5  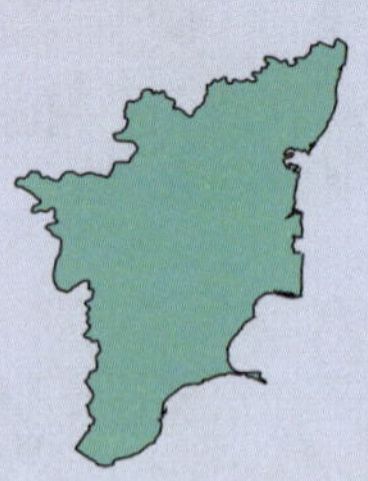

Kanchipuram silk of ....

6  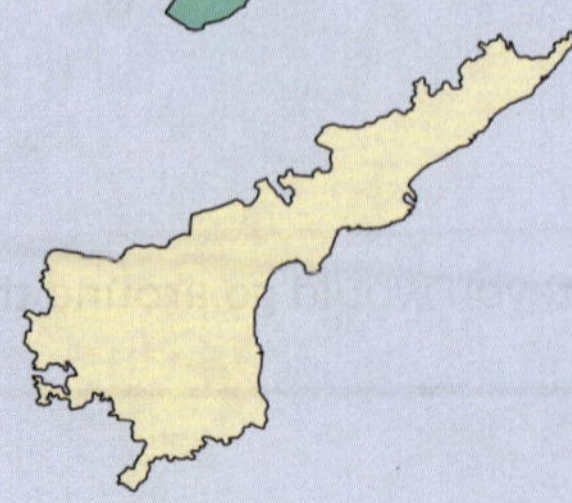

Tirupati laddu of ....

7

Bastar dhokra, metalcraft of

....

8

Muga silk of

....

9

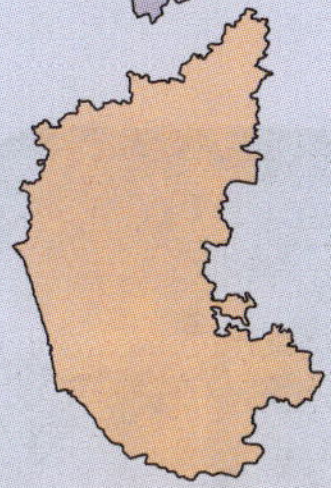

Bidriware of

....

10

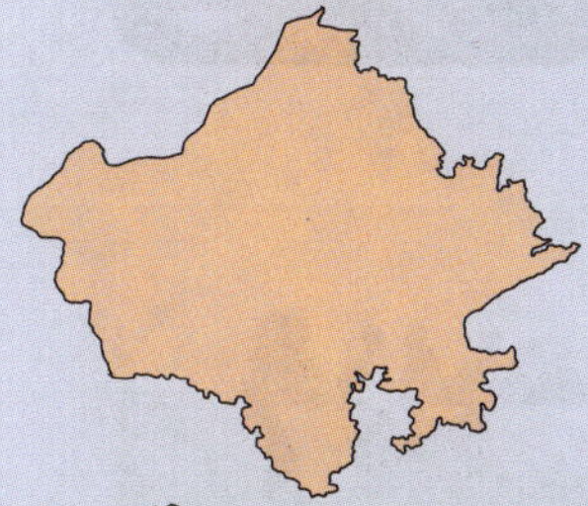

Kathputlis (cloth puppets) of

....

11

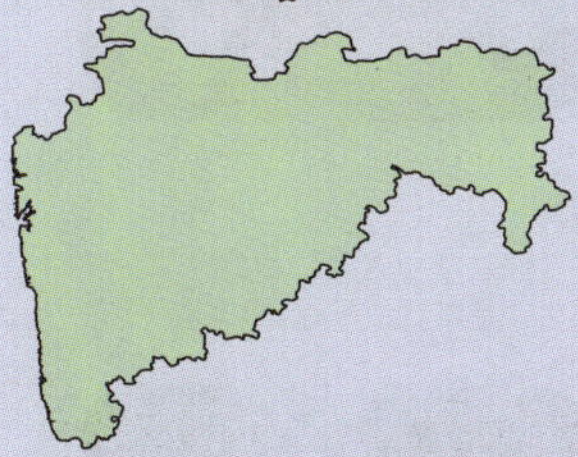

Kolhapuri chappals of

....

12

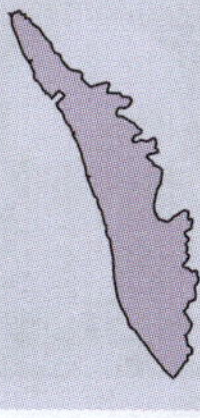

Wayanad robusta coffee from

....

Help box

Odisha | Andhra Pradesh | Assam | Rajasthan | Madhya Pradesh | Bihar | Tamil Nadu | Jammu and Kashmir | Chhattisgarh | Karnataka | Maharashtra | Kerala

Whiz fact

The city of Mysuru (Mysore) is linked with 18 different GI tagged products. These are silk, *agarbatti (incense sticks)*, rosewood inlay, sandalwood oil, sandal soap, traditional paintings, betel leaf, *ganjifa* cards and *Mysuru mallige* (Mysore jasmine).

STEM

38 Science of Sports

Sports equipment and techniques are based on science.

Use the pictures and match Column A to Column B to complete the statements.

Column A

1 In baseball, metal bats help the ball travel faster, but wooden bats continue to be used

2 Skaters kick off against a wall or curb to first begin moving. This illustrates Newton's third law of motion that an action has an equal and opposite reaction.

3 A golf ball has to travel a long way, at least when it is first struck. It can only do this if it reduces air resistance.

4 When a boomerang is thrown, one wing moves through the air faster than the other.

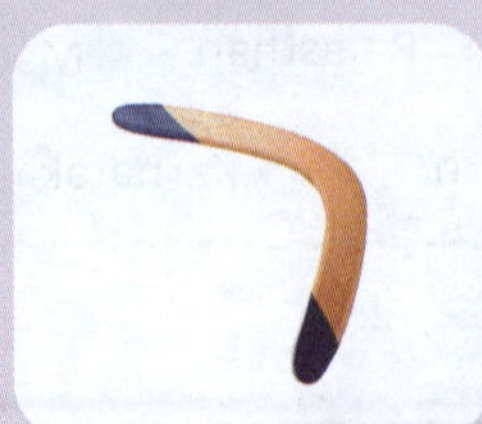

Column B

a That's why it is small and has dimples on it.

b As the top wing spins forward, the lift force on it is greater than that on the lower wing. This imbalance in force is what causes it to turn and come back.

c That's why they kick backward so that they can move forward.

d because it focuses the game on the skill of the players. It also keeps spectators safer.

5 Olympic swimmers wear very fitted bodysuits,

6 Cyclists bend over their bikes till they are almost horizontal and wear helmets shaped like a teardrop.

7 When a football player kicks a ball off-centre, the ball spins. How much the ball curves depends on the direction and speed of the spin.

8 Divers tuck their arms and legs in after they spring off the board. They do their somersaults in this way to preserve their angular momentum.

e Only then do they extend their arms to enter the water safely without causing a splash.

f The curve of the ball as it flies is called the Magnus effect.

g so that their body offers minimum resistance to water, which is relatively dense.

h This minimises their surface area, therefore minimising air resistance, and allows them to move faster.

Whiz quiz

Choose the correct option.

All sports involve force. Athletes would not be able to run/swim without the force of friction to prevent their feet from slipping. While playing video games/ball, a force applied to it makes it move, whether from the kick of a footballer or the action of a tennis racquet. While cycling, force makes the tyres/vehicles move and other forces are needed to stop them.

Whiz fact

For a tennis player to generate a spin, he or she has to start with the racquet at the waist, bring it up and forward and twist with the hips and elbow. The racquet must brush across the ball and the head of the racquet must finish high above the opposite shoulder.

Literacy Skills

39 How Cinema Developed

MEDIA

The Bioscope was the first movie projector invented and the first film ever shown consisted of a number of very short films of about six seconds each, which were shown repeatedly a number of times.

Use the words in the help box to solve this crossword related to cinema.

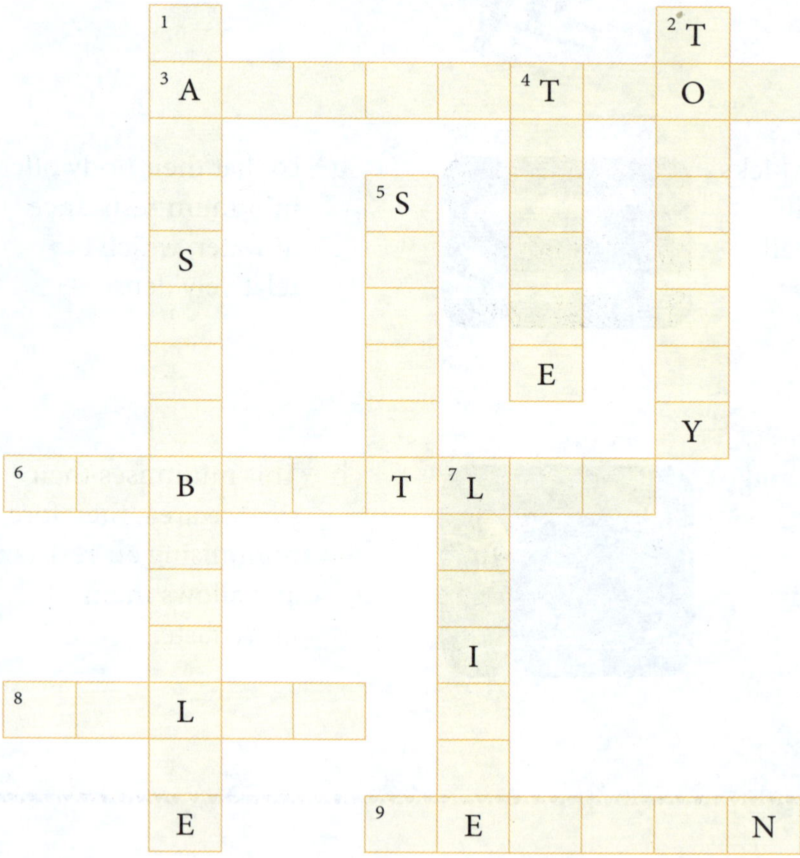

Across

3 This type of film shows moving cartoons. *Little Nemo*, a 2-minute silent film hand-coloured frame by frame, is the first such movie to have been made.

6 Silent films showed .... to help viewers understand what was happening on screen. Today, these are called intertitles.

8 Stanley Kubrick's 1971 film A *Clockwork Orange* was the first film to use this sound technology.

9 The first real film was shown here by Max Skladanowsky in July 1895.

Down

1 The first Indian filmmaker who made a film called *Raja Harishchandra* in 1913. The highest award in cinema in India today is named after him.

2 The first fully computer-generated feature film, made by Pixar founder John Lasseter

4 A film with sound was called ....

5 Earlier films, which had no dialogues, were called .... films.

7 These French brothers began showing films in December 1895.

Whiz quiz

Write the names of the following:

1 India's first film: ....

2 First full-length motion picture released in India: ....

3 First chain of Indian cinemas: ....

Whiz fact

The first Indian colour film was V Shantaram's *Sairandhri* but it was processed and printed in Germany. The 1937 film *Kisan Kanya*, produced by Ardeshir Irani, is thus considered the first true Indian colour film as it was made in India.

40 Immortal Words

Some speeches are remembered and quoted decades or even centuries after they were made.

Match the speakers with their immortal words.

1 

Queen Elizabeth I

2 

Rabindranath Tagore

3 

Nelson Mandela

4 

Bal Gangadhar Tilak

a In May 1941, a Nobel laureate from India on his eightieth birthday said, "As I look around I see the crumbling ruins of a proud civilisation strewn like a vast heap of futility."

b In April 1917, at the first anniversary of the Home Rule League in Nashik, an Indian freedom fighter said, "Freedom is my birthright. So long as it is awake within me, I am not old. No weapon can cut this spirit, no fire can burn it."

c In July 1588, in a speech to the troops at the Tilbury Camp, a British monarch said, "Any prince of Europe, should dare to invade the borders of my realm .... I myself will take up arms—I myself will be your general, judge and rewarder of every one of your virtues in the field."

d In May 1994, in Johannesburg, South Africa, a famous world leader said, "You have shown such a calm, patient determination to reclaim this country as your own. And joy that we can loudly proclaim from the rooftops—Free at Last!"

5 

Abraham Lincoln

6 

Michelle Obama

7 

Jawaharlal Nehru

8 

Martin Luther King Jr.

e In 2008, at the Democratic National Convention, a famous lawyer and writer said, "We learned about dignity and decency—that how hard you work matters more than how much you make ... that helping others means more than just getting ahead yourself."

f On 28 August, 1963 at the Lincoln Memorial, Washington DC, a civil rights activist said, "I have a dream that my four little children will one day live in a nation where they will not be judged by the colour of their skin, but by the content of their character. I have a dream today!"

g On 19 November, 1863 at Gettysburg, Pennsylvania, USA, a US President said, "... and that government of the people, by the people, for the people, shall not perish from the earth."

h At midnight between 14th and 15th August, 1947, an Indian statesman said, "Long years ago we made a tryst with destiny and now the time comes when we shall redeem our pledge, not wholly or in full measure, but very substantially."

Whiz fact

George Washington was not a fan of public speaking. The speech that opened his presidency was amongst the shortest on record. He delivered it in 135 words, about one minute!

41 The Sound of Music

Music adds so much value to storytelling that most film awards recognise original music and songs of films.

Match these songs and singers with the movies in which they feature.

Songs and Singers

1. *Hakuna Matata* meaning 'No Worries' is a Swahili language song sung by Jimmy Cliff and Lebo M in this movie about Simba.
2. *I Like to Move It* is a song from a movie in which zoo animals escape to an island off the coast of Africa. It is sung by Real 2 Reel and The Mad Stuntman
3. *Let It Go*, pictured on the character Elsa, is sung by Idina Menzel
4. *I See the Light* sung by Mandy Moore, is a song from a movie inspired by the fairytale Rapunzel, with new characters, villains and several twists.
5. *Happy* sung by Pharrell Williams is a single from the second film in this animated film series. The series itself is the most successful animated film franchise ever, with its little yellow beings and the supervillain Gru.

Movies

a 

Madagascar

b 

Despicable Me 2

c 

Tangled

d 

Frozen

e 

The Lion King

6 *We Belong Together* sung by Randy Newman is an award-winning song from the third movie of this franchise, featuring Woody, Buzz and their friends.

7 *Down to Earth* sung by Peter Gabriel features in a movie about a garbage-cleaning robot in the year 2805, who travels across the galaxy.

8 *Good Foot* sung by Justin Timberlake plays in an underwater animated film about a boastful fish named Oscar.

9 *Le Festin* sung by Camille and composed by Michael Giacchino plays in this unforgettable story about a little rodent chef named Rémi.

10 *Purple People Eater* sung by Sheb Wooley plays in a whimsical story of a 'one-eyed, one-horned, flying purple people eater' who comes to Earth to join a rock 'n' roll band.

f 

Ratatouille

g 

Shark Tale

h 

Toy Story

i 

Monsters vs. Aliens

j 

WALL-E

Whiz fact

Alan Menken, who composed the music for *The Little Mermaid*, *Beauty and the Beast*, *Aladdin*, *Pocahontas* and *Tangled*, has won eight Oscars.

India Focus

42 The Indian Navy

The Indian Navy is the naval branch of the Indian Armed Forces. The President of India is the Supreme Commander of the Indian Navy. The Chief of Naval Staff, a four-star admiral, commands the navy.

Use the clues and the help box to identify and fill in the names of some ships of the Indian Navy in the blanks given.

1. .... is an aircraft carrier that was formerly called the Admiral Gorshkov and is now named after a great Indian king.
2. .... is a Shivalik-class frigate named after one of the constituent ranges of the Western Ghats.

3. .... is the Indian Navy's *Akula*-class nuclear-powered submarine. Its name occurs in the Indian emblem.
4. .... is an example of a *Sukanya*-class patrol vessel and is named after the legendary wife of Satyavan.

5. All the Kilo-class diesel submarines of the Indian Navy have names that begin with a six-letter word ...., which is the Sanskrit name of the river Indus.
6. .... is a type of frigate named after the Hindi word for sword.

7. .... is a Brahmaputra-class frigate named after a river that flows through Himachal Pradesh and Punjab.
8. .... is the smallest type of warship named after the traditional knife used by Gurkha warriors.

Help box

INS Savitri | Sindhu | INS Beas | INS Khukri | INS Chakra | INS Sahyadri | INS Vikramaditya | INS Talwar

Whiz fact

The INS Vikrant is India's first indigenous aircraft carrier and the largest and most complex warship built in the country. The 40,000-tonne warship stationed in the Arabian Sea is a testimony to India's engineering prowess and a symbol of Atmanirbhar Bharat.

43 Airports

Countries, cities and roads are named after famous people and so are airports. Given below are some airports named after famous people along with the cities or towns in which they are located.
Pick the correct location from the given options.

1 The João Paulo II Airport named after Pope John Paul II is in Seville, Spain/Ponta Delgada, Portugal.

2 The Il Caravaggio International Airport is in Katowice, Poland/Bergamo, Italy.

3 The Madeira International Airport Cristiano Ronaldo is in Portugal/Italy.

4 Dr Babasaheb Ambedkar International Airport is in Nagpur, India/Chittagong, Bangladesh.

5 The Venice Marco Polo Airport is in Italy/France.

6 The Istanbul Ataturk Airport is in Morocco/Turkey.

7 The Tribhuvan International Airport is in Punakha, Bhutan/Kathmandu, Nepal.

8 The Liverpool John Lennon Airport is in Liverpool, England/Liverpool, New York.

9 The Salzburg Airport W A Mozart is in Germany/Austria.

10 The Julius Nyerere International Airport is in Dar es Salaam, Tanzania/Accra, Ghana.

11 The Simón Bolívar International Airport is in Buenos Aires, Argentina/Maiquetía, Venezuela.

Whiz fact

Ian Fleming, creator of the *James Bond* spy novels, was a Londoner and part-time resident of Jamaica. In 2011, the airport at Boscobel in Jamaica was renamed the Ian Fleming Airport. Many protested as they felt the honour should have gone to a Jamaican.

STEM

44 Cells in the Body

The cell is the basic unit of living organisms. There are hundreds of different types of cells in the body and the structure of each is perfectly suited to the role it performs.

Match Column A with Column B to learn more about cells.

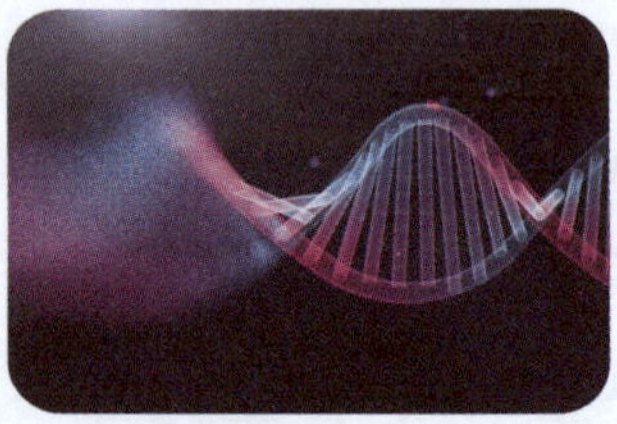

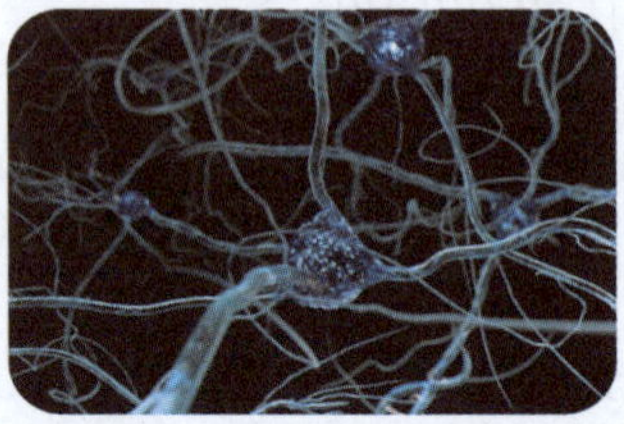

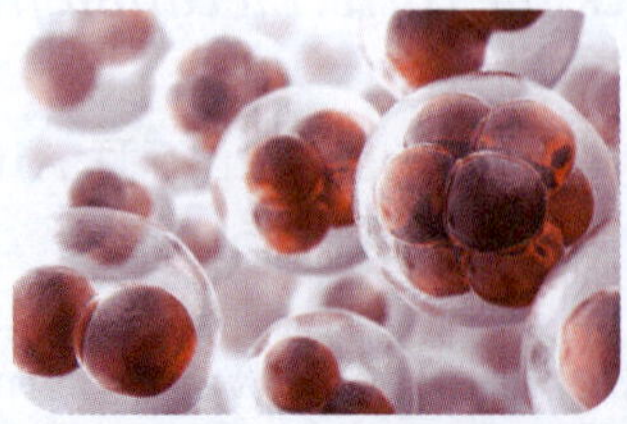

Column A	Column B
1 Platelets	a are reproductive cells.
2 Gametes	b are colourless cell fragments in our blood that form clots and stop bleeding.
3 Single-celled organisms	c have the ability to contract in order to produce movement of the body parts.
4 Epithelial cells, like skin cells and mucus	d carry oxygen to the body's tissues and collect carbon dioxide.
5 Neurons	e protect the internal structures of the body from damage, prevent dehydration and act as a barrier against germs.
6 Blood cells	f send signals among the brain, spinal cord and other body organs.
7 Muscle cells	g are called unicellular.

Whiz fact

Cancer cells are created by mutations that occur due to chemicals, radiation, ultraviolet light, chromosome replication errors or viral infection. Cancer cells lose the ability to undergo programmed cell death.

45 Suffixes that Suffice

Some words have words added after them.
The words added after are called suffixes.

SUFFIX

Given below are ten words with their meanings. Each word uses a suffix.

1. Theology – the study of God and divinity
2. Trigonometry – the measurement of land through triangles
3. Kingdom – a country, state or territory ruled by a king or queen
4. Astigmatism – the condition of being nearsighted
5. Cardiology – the study of diseases and abnormalities of the heart, and their treatment
6. beautify – to make beautiful
7. Activism – a policy of action to achieve a political or social goal
8. Zoometry – the branch of zoology that measures the relative length or size of the different parts of an animal or animals
9. Freedom – the power or right to act, speak or think as one wants
10. Simplify – to make simple

Choose the correct meaning of each suffix given below.

1. metry
   - a the process of measuring ☐
   - b mastery over something ☐
2. logy
   - a study of a subject ☐
   - b related to tree trunks ☐
3. ism
   - a related to being-ness ☐
   - b condition, doctrine, action ☐
4. ify
   - a being unsure ☐
   - b to make or become ☐
5. dom
   - a place or state of being ☐
   - b related to beingness ☐

Whiz fact

The suffix *athon* was extracted from the word 'marathon' in the 1930s, so now we have danceathons, bakeathons, telethons and other such events!

46 Jewels of India

India Focus

The Bharat Ratna can be translated as the 'Jewel of India'. It is the highest civilian award given by the Government of India.

Match the Bharat Ratna awardees with the exceptional services or performances for which they were given the award.

1. Amartya Sen

2. M S Subbulakshmi

3. Aruna Asaf Ali

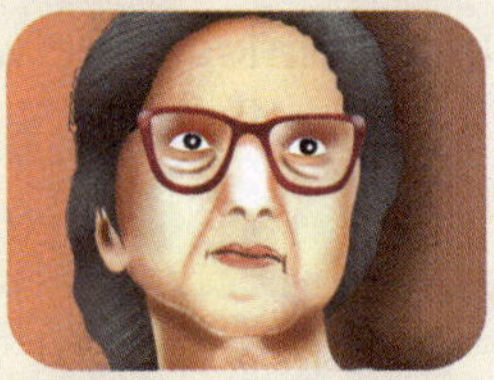

4. B R Ambedkar

5. A P J Abdul Kalam

6. Vinoba Bhave

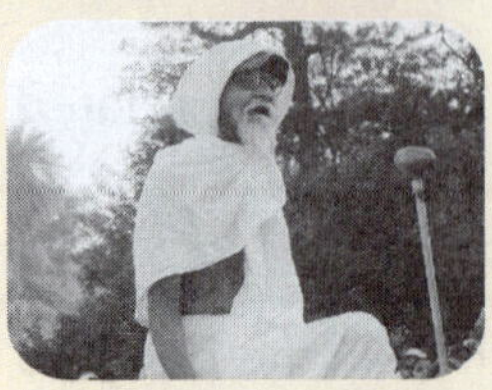

a. He was India's first law minister and the chief architect of the Constitution of India.

b. An aerospace scientist known for his scientific mind, he entered public life late in life.

c. A renowned Carnatic vocalist and the first musician on whom the Bharat Ratna was conferred.

d. One of the world's most renowned economists, he was also awarded the Nobel Prize for Economics.

e. This human rights activist is best known for starting the *Bhoodan* Movement.

f. An important leader of the Quit India Movement, she became the first woman Mayor of Delhi in 1958. She was also given the Lenin Peace Prize in 1965.

7 Satyajit Ray

8 Mother Teresa

9 Indira Gandhi

10 Jehangir Ratanji Dadabhoy Tata

11 Ravi Shankar

12 Lata Mangeshkar

g An industrialist, philanthropist and aviation pioneer, he founded India's first airline, Air India.

h A legendary Indian playback singer, she started singing at the age of 13. She recorded songs for over a thousand Hindi films.

i A sitar player, he won four Grammy Awards and is known for his collaborative work with Western musicians like violinist Yehudi Menuhim and George Harrison.

j A famous missionary, she came to India from North Macedonia, then a part of the Ottoman Empire. She began teaching at St. Mary's High School in Kolkata but gave up her job to dedicate her life to helping the poor.

k An acclaimed filmmaker, author and illustrator, he directed the *Apu Trilogy*, amongst other films.

l She is the only woman Prime Minister India has had thus far. She is also remembered as one of the most formidable leaders of the Indian National Congress.

Whiz fact

Usually conferred on India-born citizens, the Bharat Ratna has been awarded to one naturalised citizen, Mother Teresa, a Pakistan national, Khan Abdul Ghaffar Khan and former South African President, Nelson Mandela.

Art and Entertainment

47 And the Oscar Goes To...

The Academy Award for Best Picture is one of the Academy Awards presented annually by the Academy of Motion Picture Arts and Sciences since the awards debuted in 1929.

Use the descriptions and help box to fill in the blanks with the names of these films.

	Descriptions	Answers
1	This much-loved 1965 musical tells the story of an aspiring nun who is sent as governess to take care of seven motherless children.	....
2	This 1997 James Cameron film starring Leonardo di Caprio and Kate Winslet tells the epic story of a ship on its maiden voyage.	....
3	This 2008 film tells the story of a teenager from the slums of Mumbai who becomes a contestant on a reality quiz show on TV.	....
4	This movie is based on a great leader of India, and won the Oscar in 1983.	....
5	This 1993 film tells the story of a German industrialist and member of the Nazi party who tries to save his Jewish employees after witnessing the persecution of Jews in Poland.	....
6	This film, the first in a trilogy, told the story of an Italian American gangster, but so compellingly, that it nearly always tops any list of great films of the 20th century.	....
7	This Tom Cruise and Dustin Hoffman film tells the poignant story of two brothers, one of whom is autistic.	....

8 A 1964 musical, based on George Bernard Shaw's play *Pygmalion*, about a Professor of Phonetics who teaches a flower girl to speak 'proper English'! ....

9 This 1959 epic, starring Charlton Heston and based on the times of Jesus Christ, was the most expensive film of its time. ....

10 Third in a trilogy based on the works of JRR Tolkien, this epic fantasy adventure won all 11 Academy Awards for which it was nominated. ....

11 This 1968 musical drama was based on Charles Dickens' famous tale of an orphan boy in gritty, grimy, industrial age London. ....

12 A 2021 coming-of-age film about a 'child of deaf adults', unusually released on OTT rather than the big screen. ....

Help box

CODA | My Fair Lady | The Lord of the Rings: The Return of the King | Gandhi | Schindler's List | *Oliver!* | The Godfather | Titanic | The Sound of Music | Ben-Hur | Rain Man | Slumdog Millionaire

Whiz fact

The 2016 musical *La La Land* received a record 14 Academy Awards nominations, tying with *All About Eve* and *Titanic*, and won 6. In a moment of confusion, it was also announced as Best Picture (read out of a duplicate card for Best Actress, which had gone to Emma Stone in *La La Land*), and the usual acknowledgment speeches had already begun before the show producers went into panic and corrected the error; the actual winner was *Moonlight*.

Literacy Skills

48 Cryptocurrency

FINANCIAL LITERACY

Read this text about cryptocurrency and fill in the blanks using the help box.

1. Cryptocurrency, also known as crypto, is a collection of binary data which is designed to work as a medium of exchange. Units are most commonly referred to as ....

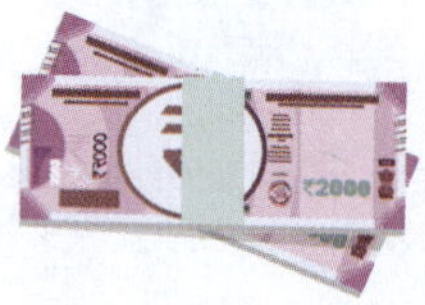

2. Cryptocurrency does not exist in physical form (like.................................... money) and is normally not issued by a central bank.

3. A cryptocurrency is a digital form of money, built on .... technology that only exists online. It uses encryption to authenticate and protect transactions.

4. ...., which was originally released in 2009, is the first such cryptocurrency. Today, there are over a thousand different cryptocurrencies in the world.

5. In June 2021, the Central American nation of .... became the first country to accept Bitcoin as legal currency. However, several countries have banned cryptocurrencies around the world.

EL SALVADOR FLAG

6. The validity of each cryptocurrency's coins is provided by a blockchain which is a continuously growing list of records or ...., which are linked and secured using cryptography.

7 In cryptocurrency networks, ... is a validation of transactions. For this effort, successful miners obtain new cryptocurrency as a reward.

8 Cryptocurrencies are used primarily outside existing banking and governmental institutions and are exchanged over the ....

9 By definition, a cryptocurrency is pseudonymous rather than anonymous in that the cryptocurrency within a .... is not tied to people, but rather to one or more specific .... (or "addresses"). Thus, the owner is not identifiable, but all transactions are publicly available in the blockchain.

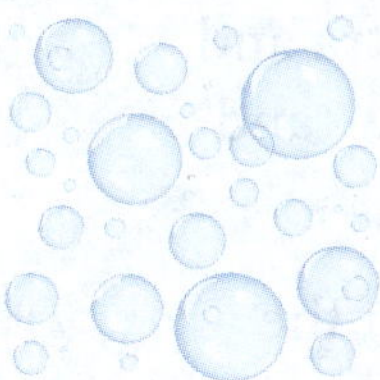

10 Its critics have called it a '............................' and compared it to the .... Mania and the Dot Com bubble.

11 Furthermore, mining for certain cryptocurrencies consumes significant quantities of .... and has a large carbon ....

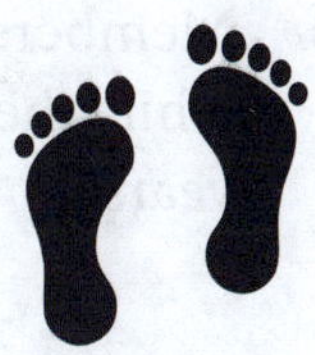

Help box

El Salvador | coins | paper | mining | wallet | blocks | Bitcoin
internet | Tulip | electricity | bubble | blockchain | footprint | keys

Whiz fact

Apart from Bitcoin, some popular and well-known cryptocurrencies include Ethereum, (ETH), Litecoin (LTC), Cardano (ADA), Polkadot (DOT) and Dogecoin (DOGE).

49 Electoral System of India

India is a sovereign, socialist, secular, democratic republic. The Constitution of India adopted a Parliamentary form of government.

Read the statements and fill in the blanks with words from the help box.

1. The Parliament consists of the .... and the two houses—Lok Sabha and ....
2. India is divided into .... parliamentary constituencies. Members of parliament, one from each constituency, make up the ....
3. Each state and union territory has its own assemblies, called the ....
4. In the six states of Andhra Pradesh, Telangana, Bihar, Karnataka, Maharashtra and Uttar Pradesh, the state legislature consists of the .... and two houses—the .... and the legislative assembly.
5. 22 states and a few union territories have their state legislatures consisting of the Governor and the state ....
6. Members of the Lok Sabha are elected for a term of .... years while the members of the Rajya Sabha are elected for a term of .... years.

Help box

legislative assembly | five | President of India | 543
Rajya Sabha | Vidhan Sabha | legislative council
six | Governor | Lok Sabha

Whiz fact

The Election Commission of India is an autonomous constitutional authority responsible for administering Union and State election processes in India. It administers all elections, including those to the offices of the President and the Vice President of India.

World Around Us

50 The Islands of Zanzibar

Zanzibar is a semi-autonomous region of Tanzania. It is an archipelago in the Indian Ocean and consists of many small islands and two large ones—Unguja or Zanzibar and Pemba.

Use the help box to fill in the blanks to learn some interesting facts about Zanzibar.

1. The islands of Zanzibar are often called the .... because of the production and export of cloves, cinnamon, black pepper and nutmeg.
2. The official languages of Zanzibar are English, ... and ....
3. From ancient times, Zanzibar was seen as a gateway to mainland East Africa and throughout history, the .... , the .... , the Omani and the British have fought to control the island.
4. The capital of Zanzibar is Zanzibar City. Its historic centre is a UNESCO World Heritage Site called ....
5. Zanzibar is the home of the endangered Kirk's red colobus ....
6. Chumber Island is a protected marine park where visitors can snorkel to enjoy the .... of Zanzibar.
7. The existence of the subspecies Zanzibar servaline genet was discovered recently in 1995, which is why its conservation status is ....
8. .... , the lead singer of the popular rock and roll band Queen, was born in Zanzibar in 1946.

Help box

Freddie Mercury | spice islands | Stone Town | coral reefs | Swahili | Portuguese | Arabic | monkey | uncertain | Persians

Whiz fact

The shortest war in history broke out between the United Kingdom and Zanzibar on 27 August 1896. It lasted all of 38 minutes!

Sports

51 Records for All Time

Records are made and broken all the time in the world of sports. But there have been a few unmatched sporting performances.

Match the Sportspersons with their achievements by filling in the blanks with their names.

Achievements		Sportsperson
1 This bowler from England took nineteen wickets at the 1956 Ashes test match. He is the first player to take all ten wickets in a test match innings.		....
2 This tennis player from Germany was ranked number one in women's tennis by the Women's Tennis Association (WTA) for a record 377 weeks.		....
3 This former world number one squash player from Pakistan holds the world record for the longest winning streak. He won 555 matches consecutively between 1981 and 1986.		....
4 This French football player holds the record of scoring the maximum number of goals in a single edition of the FIFA World Cup. He scored thirteen goals in just six matches during the 1958 World Cup.		....
5 This Romanian gymnast became the first gymnast to score the maximum possible score, a 'perfect 10', at the 1976 Montreal Olympics.		....

6 In 1954, this athlete from England became the first person to run a mile in less than four minutes (3 minutes 59.4 seconds), then considered a physically impossible task.

....

7 This British rower is the only person to have won gold medals at five different Olympic Games.

....

8 This US swimmer won a total of 23 Olympic gold medals including a record eight gold medals at the 2008 Beijing Olympics.

....

9 This American athlete broke four world records in less than an hour on 25 May 1935 at the Big Ten Championships, a feat that has never been repeated. He did this despite a back injury!

....

Help box

Jahangir Khan | Jim Laker | Just Fontaine | Steffi Graf | Nadia Comăneci | Jesse Owens | Michael Phelps | Sir Roger Bannister | Sir Steve Redgrave

Whiz quiz

Write the names of these famous athletes.

1 Jamaican sprinting legend who won 8 Olympic golds: ....

2 Brazilian who was IOC's Sportsman of the Century, 1999: ....

Whiz fact

Brazilian football legend Pele scored 127 goals in 1959, the maximum ever scored by a football player in a calendar year.

52 Mesopotamia

The Mesopotamian civilisation formed on the banks of the Tigris and Euphrates rivers almost 10,000 years ago in what is now Iraq.

Use the help box and fill in the blanks to understand the story of the ancient Mesopotamian civilisation.

1 The Sumerian civilisation which took form in about 4000 BCE developed .... in 3000 BCE, one of the first written scripts consisting of wedge-shaped marked pressed into clay tablets.

2 The ...., one of the world's first great works of literature, was written in this script.

3 Sumerians are credited with the incredibly important invention of the .... as early as 3500 BCE and images of chariots are evidence of this.

4 Sumerians used a .... to denote ownership of property and to stand for an individual's signature. It was comparable to one's modern-day identification card.

5 The Mesopotamian civilisation is characterised by the ...., a massive terraced compound made with sun-baked and fired bricks, built of successively receding stories or levels.

6 Around 3000 BCE, the Sumerians had significant cultural interaction with the Akkadians in northern Mesopotamia. The Akkadian language is related to the modern .... languages of Hebrew and Arabic.

7 Around 2334 BCE, ... of Akkad came to power and established what might have been the world's first dynastic empire, ruling over both Akkadian and Sumerian speakers in Mesopotamia and the .... in modern-day Syria and Lebanon.

8 The empire of Akkad collapsed within 180 years of its founding and from the late 21st century BCE till the late 7th century BCE, the .... were the dominant power in the north of Mesopotamia.

9 .... was a minor city-state in central Mesopotamia for a century after it was founded in 1894 BCE. The reign of Hammurabi made it the most powerful empire in the world.

10 ...., written on stone slabs called *stele* and clay tablets, is one of the oldest deciphered writing of significant length in the world. It is the basis of many laws codified even in modern times.

11 The Babylonian Empire was sacked by invaders in 1531 BCE and reasserted itself in 626 BCE, till it was overthrown in 539 BCE by the .... who then ruled over the region until the time of Alexander the Great in 335 BCE.

Help box

Hammurabi's Code | cuneiform | Semitic | Assyrians | cylinder seal | *Epic of Gilgamesh* | Babylon | Persians | wheel | Sargon | Levant | Ziggurat of Ur

Whiz Fact

Mesopotamia is the birthplace of modern civilisation. Since it was located at the crossroads of the Egyptian and the Indus Valley civilisations, it became a melting pot of languages and cultures.

Sports

53 The Story of Tennis

Read the story of how tennis developed into the game it is today.

1 Tennis is believed to have originated in the 12th century in Northern France. The ball was struck with the palm of the hand, which is why it was called *jeu de paume*, or 'game of the palm'. It was popular with Louis X and King Charles V.

2 In the 16th century, racquets began to be used. When a person served, they usually called out the French word *tenez*, which means 'hold' or 'take'. This led to the game being called 'tennis'. Tennis was popular in France and England.

3 The patenting of the lawn mower in 1830 in Britain paved the way for the preparation of modern-style grass courts. In 1872, the world's first tennis club was founded in Birmingham, where the phrase 'lawn tennis' was first used.

4 In December 1873, the rules that developed into modern tennis were developed. This led to the creation of a boxed set that included a net, poles, racquets and balls, which was sold all over the world along with the rules.

5 The world's oldest annual tennis tournament took place at Leamington Lawn Tennis Club in Birmingham in 1874.

6 Three years later, the All England Lawn Tennis and Croquet Club held its first championships at Wimbledon in 1877. This was the first ever Wimbledon Championship held.

7 In 1874, socialite Mary Ewing Outerbridge laid out a tennis court at Staten Island, New York. The first American National Championship was played there in September 1880.

8 In 1881, the oldest nationwide tennis organisation in the world, the United States Lawn Tennis Association, was formed. It is now called the United States Tennis Association. The US National Men's Singles Championships, now called the US Open, were held in 1881, while the US National Women's Singles Championships were first held in 1887.

9 The French Championships began in 1891, though till 1925, it was open only to tennis players who were members of French clubs. The Australian Open began in 1905.

Now, say whether the following statements are true or false by marking T or F against each one.

1. Some tennis terms, in fact, even the name of the game itself, show that the sport originated in France.
2. The lawn mower paved the way for the preparation of modern-style hard courts.
3. The world's first tennis club was founded in 1872 in London.
4. In 1874, socialite Mary Ewing Outerbridge laid out a tennis court in Birmingham.
5. The first US National Women's Singles Championships were first held in 1881.

Whiz quiz

Here are the names of two famous tennis champions, one male and the other female. Unscramble the letters to find their names.

Female: NESEAR LAMISLIW

....

Male: ERGRO DEFREER

....

Whiz fact

One interesting theory about the term 'love', used to denote a score of zero in tennis, is that it originated from the French word for 'egg'. A zero resembles the shape of an egg and 'egg' is called *l'oeuf* in French, hence the term 'love'!

54 Performing Arts of India

India has many performing arts performed by its diverse tribes, clans and regions. The stories, style, costumes, accompaniment and embellishment make each one an experience to savour.

Use the names provided in the help box to find the names of traditional performing arts in India. Fill in the blanks with the names of the performing arts.

1 This dramatic folk theatre form from Uttar Pradesh involves the reenactment of the life of Lord *Rama*. It is staged annually over many days and culminates on the auspicious day of *Dussehra* or *Vijayadashmi*.
....

2 This folk singing theatre form involves narrating tales from the *Mahabharata*. It is popular in Chhattisgarh and its neighbouring areas.
....

3 An operatic theatre form from Uttar Pradesh, it is characterised by sharp dialogues, melodrama, declamation, singing and dancing.
....

4 This folk theatre is performed during temple festivals in Tamil Nadu. The name roughly translates to street play in Tamil. The themes are usually from the *Mahabharata*. ....

5 Also known as Vesha or Swang, this popular folk theatre form from Gujarat is partly entertainment and partly a ritual offering made to Goddess *Amba*. ....

6 This ancient Urdu storytelling form which was popular in North India essentially means to tell a tale in Persian. There is no acting; all the theatrics lie in the voice and delivery of the storyteller, who performs while sitting. ....

7 This 18th century Marathi theatre form involves singing and dancing. Its name means commotion in Urdu, Hindi and Marathi. ....

8 This Sanskrit theatre form of Kerala deals with plays of eminent Sanskrit dramatists such as Bhasa, Harsha, Kalidasa, Mahendravikrama and Saktibhadra. ....

9 The name of this highly energetic theatre form comes from two words meaning nature spirits and song. It is predominantly performed in Karnataka and parts of Kerala. ....

10 Literally meaning procession or journey, this folk theatre form from Bengal came into being as a result of the Bhakti Movement, in which devotees of Krishna sang and danced in processions. ....

Help box

Tamasha	Koodiyattam	Yakshagana	Jatra	Therukoothu
Bhavai	Dastangoi	Ramlila	Pandavani	Nautanki

Whiz Fact

Bhand Pather is a traditional theatre form of Kashmir. It is a unique blend of dance, music and acting. Satire, wit and parody are used in this folk drama that incorporates local mythological legends and contemporary social commentary.

Sports

55 The Paralympic Games

The Paralympic Games were created so that athletes with physical disabilities could participate in sports at the international level. The first edition of the Paralympic Games was held in 1960 in Rome. Paris hosted the 2024 Games for the first time from 28 August to 8 September. Unusually, the logo of the Paralympic Games was exactly the same as that of the Olympics for non-disabled people.

Here are some famous Paralympic champions from different countries and their achievements. Match the images with the descriptions.

1 
Mariyappan Thangavelu

2 
Ellie Simmonds

3 
Devendra Jhajharia

4 
Esther Vergeer

5 
Avani Lekhara

a. She was only 13 when she won two swimming golds in Beijing in 2008.

b. This Indian Paralympian holds two gold medals and one silver for javelin throw — in the Athens and Rio Olympics (2004 and 2016) and at the Tokyo Olympics held in 2021.

c. He used his deformed foot to his advantage and won gold in the high jump at the 2016 Paralympics.

d. She became the first Indian woman to win gold at a Paralympic event after she equalled the world record with a score of 249.6 in the women's 10m air rifle standing finals at the Tokyo Paralympics.

e. She is considered the greatest Paralympic tennis player. She won 48 grand slams. She was ranked #1 in the world from 1999 until 2013, when she retired.

Whiz Fact

1. Goalball is a paralympic sport played by athletes who are blind or visually impaired. All athletes must be legally blind, which means they have <10% vision. The athletes wear blindfolds so that the competition is fair and the ball has a bell in it so they can hear where it is. This game needs the audience to be absolutely quiet so that athletes can clearly hear the ball.
2. The mascots for the Paris Olympics as well as the Paralympics were the Phryges. Interestingly, the Phryge representing the Paralympics is shown on a running blade, the first time that a Summer Paralympics mascot is shown with a disability.

India Focus

56 Founders and Heads

Indians who move to and live in another country form the Indian diaspora. Here are some members of the Indian diaspora who are founders and heads of companies.

Match them with their achievements by writing the correct letter in the boxes.

1 

Sabeer Bhatia ☐

2 

Ajit Jain ☐

3 

Lakshmi Mittal ☐

4 

Indra Nooyi ☐

5 

Amar Bose ☐

6 

Satya Nadella ☐

a Born in Chennai and in the US now, she was until recently Chairperson and CEO of PepsiCo.

b The Chairman and CEO of ArcelorMittal, the world's second-largest steel-making company, he was born in Rajasthan and lives in the UK.

c Born in Chandigarh and living in the United States now, he founded Hotmail and sold it to Microsoft in 1997.

d Born in Bengal, this engineer founded the Bose Corporation, which he donated to MIT, where he served as Professor for 45 years.

e This CEO was born in Hyderabad and played an important role in Microsoft's cloud and infrastructure services.

f This Odisha-born person became President of the Berkshire Hathaway Reinsurance group in the United States in 2018.

Whiz Fact

As of 2023, there are more than 29 million people of Indian origin around the world, with 2.5 million being added every year, making Indian diaspora the largest number of migrants of any nation in the world.

57 The Printing Press

Before the invention of the printing press, books were produced by hand. They were written on clay, parchment wax or papyrus. Each book had to be painstakingly copied by hand to make another copy of it—till the invention of the printing press by Johannes Gutenberg between 1440 and 1450. The very first book he printed on the press was the *Bible*, prized today as the *Gutenberg Bible*.

INFORMATION

1 Between 1300s and 1400s, people used a very basic form of printing using wooden stamps. In this form of printing, letters or images are cut on blocks of wood, which are dipped in ink and then stamped onto paper.

2 Gutenberg realised that he could use cut blocks within a machine to make the printing process a lot quicker.

3 Gutenberg replaced wood blocks with metal block letters, which could be moved around within the machine to create new words. This became to be known as a 'movable type machine'.

4 In the original printing press, groups of type blocks set in reverse within a frame make words and sentences.

5 A sheet of paper is laid on the inked blocks and passed through a roller to ensure that the ink is transferred to the paper. All this is done by hand.

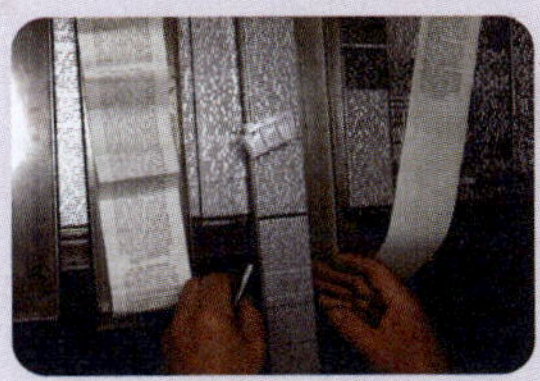

6 Because of the reversed blocks, the paper, when lifted, has normal letters.

7 Towards the 19th century, other printing presses were invented, which were steam-powered and did not require a hand operator.

8 Today were have electronic and automated printing presses that print faster than ever before.

Read these statements. Mark them T for true and F for false based on the text and pictures given above.

1 Printing existed before the invention of the printing press by Johannes Gutenberg.

2 The letters on the blocks read exactly the same as the printed letters do on paper.

3 Gutenberg used metal blocks which could be moved around within the machine to create new words and sentences.

4 Steam-powered printing presses were slower than Gutenberg's printing press.

5 First the letters are set, then blocks are inked, then a sheet of paper is laid on the blocks, and lastly, all this passes through a roller to get a sheet of printed paper.

Whiz Fact

The *Diamond Sutra*, a Buddhist book from Dunhuang, China, dating to around 868 CE during the Tang Dynasty, is said to be the oldest known printed book. Hand-carved wood blocks were used to print the letters in the book.

58 The History and Breakup of the Soviet Union

Very few short-lived nations could have matched the power and influence of the Union of Soviet Socialist Republics, called USSR or the Soviet Union. The USSR controlled a substantial chunk of world affairs in its heyday.

Using the help boxes at the end of each section, piece together this short history of the twentieth century's powerhouse nation. Warning: each box has some incorrect answers.

Pre-USSR

Peter the Great founded the Russian Empire in the 18th century, and became a (a) ...., or Emperor. Its capital city was called (b) .... after Peter the Great.

But Russia had a few very rich people and many very (c) .... people. Interestingly, in 1867, Russia sold (d) .... to USA . In 1959, it became the 49th state of USA.

Help box 1

Alaska | wealthy | Tsar | St Petersburg | poor | Moscow

The USSR is formed

In (e) ...., (f) .... Lenin led the people to fight for their rights. The Tsar of the time, Nicholas II , was removed. His city, St Petersburg was renamed Leningrad.

In 1922, the Russian Empire became the Union of Soviet Socialist Republics (USSR) or the Soviet Union. Its capital city was Moscow and its citizens followed (g) ....

Once Lenin died in 1924, (h) .... took command. He ruled the USSR until well after the (i) .... World War.

Help box 2

Second | Joseph Stalin | 1941 | 1917 | First

communism | Georgy Malenkov | Vladimir

Soviet Achievements

The Soviet Union sent the first animal, man and woman—Laika the (j) ...., Yuri Gagarin and Valentina Tereshkova—into space, and were thus pioneers in the space race.

From the end of World War II until the 1980s, there existed a state of tension between USSR and its allies in East-Central Europe on one side and Western Europe and the (k) .... on the other. This period was called the (l) ...., because although the nations were not strictly at war with one another, they were not friends either. The USSR and its friends were called (m) .... nations.

Help box 3

USA | Iron Curtain | Third World War | dog | Cold War | monkey

The curtain falls on the USSR

In 1989, the infamous (n) .... separating East Germany from West Germany was pulled down and several Iron Curtain countries threw off the Communist yoke.

The writing was on the wall for USSR; in 1991, it dissolved into 15 countries, the largest of which is (o) ....

Leningrad was re-renamed (p) ...., Stalingrad was renamed Volgograd, and Russia became a federation.

Help box 4

St Petersburg | Afghanistan | Great Wall | Berlin Wall | Uzbekistan | Russia

Whiz Fact

Ukraine is the second-largest country in Europe after Russia.

The ongoing Russo-Ukrainian War began in 2014, following Russia's occupation and annexation of Crimea. At the time of this book going to press, the war continues, with many lives and property sacrificed.

Whiz quiz

Write the names of the countries carved out of the Soviet Union.

Quiz Yourself 1

Answer these questions.

1. Which novel by Alexandre Dumas features Athos, Porthos and Aramis?
   (a) *The Three Friends* (b) *The Three Penny Opera*
   (c) *The Three Musketeers* (d) *The Three Blind Mice*
2. Which of these painters is a renowned exponent of the Cubist art movement?
   (a) Pablo Picasso (b) Leonardo da Vinci
   (c) Caravaggio (d) Salvador Dali
3. After which famous musician is the Salzburg airport in Austria named?
   (a) WA Mozart (b) F Chopin (c) JS Bach (d) L van Beethoven
4. What is the popular name of the fictional Bengali private investigator created by film director and writer Satyajit Ray?
   (a) Jatayu (b) Feluda
   (c) Byomkesh Bakshi (d) Karamchand
5. Name the American athlete who broke four world records in less than an hour, despite a back injury, at the 1936 Olympics, a feat that has never been repeated.
   (a) Florence Griffiths-Joyner (b) Ben Jonson
   (c) Carl Lewis (d) Jesse Owens
6. Who sang the song *Let It Go* from the movie Frozen?
   (a) Idina Menzel (b) Adele (c) Taylor Swift (d) Mariah Carey
7. Which American civil rights leader's famous speech begins with the lines, "I have a dream ..."?
   (a) Nelson Mandela (b) Desmond Tutu
   (c) George Floyd (d) Martin Luther King Jr.
8. What is originally an Indian symbol of good fortune meaning 'well-being' in Sanskrit?
   (a) Cross (b) Swastika (c) Peace (d) Tick
9. Which is the oldest university in the English speaking world?
   (a) Bologna (b) Cambridge (c) Oxford (d) Harvard
10. Which modern-day technology is named after an ancient Danish and Norwegian king called Harald Blatand?
    (a) Bluetooth (b) Skype (c) Bitmoji (d) Pinterest
11. Which author of Indian origin won the Booker of Bookers in 1993 and the Best of the Booker in 2008?
    (a) Aravind Adiga (b) Salman Rushdie (c) Arundhati Roy (d) Kiran Desai
12. In which country are the legendary cities of Samarkand, Bukhara and Tashkent located?
    (a) Afghanistan (b) Turkmenistan (c) Uzbekistan (d) Kazakhstan

Quiz Yourself 2

Answer these questions.

1. Which fort in Uttar Pradesh flaunts the Bundela and Maratha styles of architecture?
   (a) Agra (b) Sinhagad
   (c) Gwalior (d) Jhansi
2. Name the first Indian film that was made in India.
   (a) *Kisan Kanya* (b) *Alam Ara*
   (c) *Raja Harishchandra* (d) *Mughal-e-Azam*
3. In which archipelago is the UNESCO World Heritage Site called Stone Town located?
   (a) Seychelles (b) Maldives
   (c) Zanzibar (d) Madagascar
4. Which ancient tribal peoples living in central India, known for their colourful art, have given their name to the southern part of the supercontinent Pangaea?
   (a) Gonds (b) Bhils (c) Murias (d) Bhatras
5. Which is the largest traded cryptocurrency in the world?
   (a) Blockchain (b) Bitcoin (c) Ethereum (d) Dogecoin
6. Which primatologist is considered the world's foremost authority on apes?
   (a) Steve Irwin (b) Rachel Carson
   (c) Jane Goodall (d) Wangari Maathai
7. What is the nickname given to the Kannada film industry based in Bengaluru?
   (a) Sandalwood (b) Kollywood
   (c) Kanniwood (d) Nammawood
8. Which film starring Aamir Khan chronicles Mahavir Phogat who trains his daughters to win Olympic medals in wrestling?
   (a) *Gold* (b) *Chak De! India*
   (c) *Dangal* (d) *Sultan*
9. In which city were the 1986 Asian Games held?
   (a) New Delhi (b) Beijing (c) Kuala Lumpur (d) Seoul
10. Which town in Madhya Pradesh is a site of the Kumbh Mela?
    (a) Nashik (b) Ujjain (c) Prayagraj (d) Haridwar
11. What nickname is given to nitrous oxide, which makes people happy, and can thus be used to help patients relax before a medical procedure?
    (a) Laughing gas (b) Quicksilver (c) Happy hormone (d) Cheerful gas
12. Which is the SI unit of temperature?
    (a) Celsius (b) Fahrenheit (c) Ampere (d) Kelvin

Quiz Yourself 3

Answer these questions.

1. Who was the first sportsperson to be awarded the Bharat Ratna?
   (a) Vishwanathan Anand (b) Dhyan Chand
   (c) Milkha Singh (d) Sachin Tendulkar
2. What did a programmer named Ray Tomlinson send for the first time in 1971?
   (a) SMS (b) DM (c) Email (d) Yantra Raja
3. Which Indian startup was acquired by Walmart for $16 billion in 2018?
   (a) Flipkart (b) Snapdeal (c) Ola (d) Oyo
4. The royal family of Sweden is the Bernadotte family, named after Jean Bernadotte, a French soldier who became the monarch of Sweden. In whose army did Jean Bernadotte serve?
   (a) Victor Emmanuel (b) William of Orange
   (c) Elizabeth I (d) Napoleon
5. Which Hindi author won the International Booker Prize 2022 for her novel *Ret Samadhi*?
   (a) Jhumpa Lahiri (b) Geetanjali Shree (c) Arundhati Roy (d) Kiran Desai
6. What item of clothing, which has buttons down the front, is named after Major General James Brudenell?
   (a) Leotard (b) Mackintosh (c) Cardigan (d) Jacuzzi
7. Which Indian currency note features the Sanchi stupa on its reverse?
   (a) ₹100 (b) ₹200 (c) ₹50 (d) ₹500
8. Which German physicist proved the existence of electromagnetic waves?
   (a) Hertz (b) Einstein (c) Heisenberg (d) Pauli
9. What name does the *Arthashastra* give to a hill fort?
   (a) Mahidurg (b) Naridurg (c) Giridurg (d) Jaladurg
10. Which county is the largest landlocked country in the world?
    (a) Russia (b) Kazakhstan (c) Canada (d) China
11. What are Sumerians credited with inventing, as evidenced by pictures of chariots?
    (a) Stylus (b) I-cards (c) Bricks (d) Wheel
12. Which is the largest island in the Mediterranean Sea?
    (a) Sardinia (b) Cyprus (c) Sicily (d) Corsica

Quiz Yourself 4

Answer these questions.

1 Which express train whose name means friendship runs from Kolkata to Dhaka?
(a) Dosti (b) Yari (c) Mitrata (d) Maitree

2 Which dog from Moscow became the first living creature to travel into space in 1957?
(a) Sputnik (b) Dolly (c) Laika (d) Yana

3 What movement did Sundarlal Bahuguna begin for the conservation of the Himalayas?
(a) Chipko (b) Green Belt Movement
(c) Magnifying glass (d) Television

4 Which popular food item owes its name and origin to John Montagu, who liked to eat meat between two slices of bread as he played card games?
(a) Footlong (b) Sandwich (c) Hamburger (d) Hotdog

5 Name the SI Unit used to measure radioactivity.
(a) Curie (b) Marconi (c) Einstein (d) Becquerel

6 In which country did impressionism, the 19th century art movement, start?
(a) Italy (b) France (c) Germany (d) Netherlands

7 In which town in Karnataka is the Gol Gumbaz located?
(a) Bijapur (b) Chikmagalur (c) Hubli (d) Ballari

8 Name the folk singing theatre form that involves narrating tales from the Mahabharata.
(a) *Tamasha* (b) *Dastangoi* (c) *Pandavani* (d) *Lavani*

9 Which British mathematician is credited with inventing calculus?
(a) Ada Lovelace (b) Isaac Newton (c) Bertrand Russell (d) Lewis Carroll

10 Which Hollywood film won 11 Academy Awards, tying with the 1959 film *Ben Hur* and later matched by the 2003 film *The Lord of the Rings: The Return of the King*?
(a) *The Godfather* (b) *The Sound of Music*
(c) *La La Land* (d) *Titanic*

11 Which festival, popularly celebrated in West Bengal in autumn, has been added to the UNESCO Intangible Heritage list in 2021?
(a) Shashoti Puja (b) Noboborsho (c) Durga Puja (d) Kali Puja

12 Which black and white animal sprays a musk causing temporary blindness to the victim?
(a) Skunk (b) Raccoon (c) Badger (d) Squirrel

Answer Key

Page 9: 1. Hercule Poirot; 2. Nancy Drew; 3. Sherlock Holmes; 4. Feluda; 5. Byomkesh Bakshi; 6. Frank and Joe Hardy

Page 10: 1. *Eighty*; 2. *Three*; 3. 50; 4. *127*; 5. *One Hundred*; 6. *2001*; 7. '69; 8. *The Thousand and One*

Page 11: 1. New Delhi; 2. Thailand; 3. 1982 Asian Games, New Delhi; 4. Hiroshima; 5. 2018; 6. Kazakhstan; 7. Israel; 8. India; 9. friendship; 10. South Korea

Page 12: 1. registered; 2. tick; 3. power; 4. peace; 5. pink ribbon; 6. swastika; 7. cross

Page 13: 1. insulin; 2. electron; 3. polio; 4. stem cells; 5. DNA; 6. kidney; 7. heart; 8. test tube; 9. Dolly

Page 14-15: 1. iii b; 2. i d; 3. iv a; 4. ii c 5. viii g; 6. vii e; 7. v h; 8. vi f

Page 16-17: 1. Switzerland; 2. Mongolia; 3. South Sudan; 4. Vatican City; 5. Paraguay; 6. Botswana; 7. Hungary; 8. Uzbekistan; 9. Nepal; 10. Laos

Page 18: 1. Lalbagh Botanical Garden; 2. IISc; 3. Vidhana Soudha; 4. Ramanagara; 5. Kempegowda; 6. Namma; 7. HAL; 8. Sandalwood; 9. Infosys; 10. Mysore

Page 19: 1. c; 2. f; 3. a; 4. e; 5. g; 6. h; 7. b; 8. d

Page 20-21: 1. Ujjain; 2. Naya Raipur; 3. Khajuraho; 4. Bilaspur; 5. Narmada; 6. Bhilai; 7. Indore; 8. Gond

Page 22-23: 1. DDT; 2. Chipko; 3. Crocodile; 4. Sequoia; 5. Peace; 6. India; 7. chimpanzees; 8. *Whale*; 9. Amazon

Page 24-25: 1. elongated, vivid colours; 2. natural shifting; 3. dots, blend in at a distance to form recognisable forms and shapes; 4. objective reality; 5. geometric figures; 6. strange; 7. spontaneity, splattering paint; 8. modern pop culture

Page 26-27: 1. d; 2. e; 3. a; 4. b; 5. c; 6. h; 7. f; 8. i; 9. g

Page 28-29: Across: 4. Naukri; 7. Make My Trip; 9. Ola; 10. Oyo; 11. Paytm

Down: 1. Snapdeal; 2. Flipkart; 3. BigBasket; 5. Just Dial; 6. Zomato; 8. Yatra

Page 30: 1. e; 2. c; 3. a; 4. f; 5. d; 6. b

Page 31: 1. 3rd Century; 2. Madhya Pradesh, *Kark Rekha*; 3. Buddhism, British; 4. Bodhi, lotuses

Page 32-33: 1. Pythagoras; 2. Euclid; 3. Gauss; 4. Newton; 5. Fibonacci; 6. Descartes; 7. Pascal

Page 34-35: 1. d; 2. f; 3. b; 4. a; 5. c; 6. e; 7. i; 8. l; 9. k; 10. g; 11. h; 12. j

Page 36: 1. Apennines; 2. Garibaldi; 3. Latin; 4. Colosseum; 5. Sicily; 6. Dante; 7. Maserati; 8. Ionian; 9. Opera; 10. Venice

Page 37: 1. Jhansi; 2. Gwalior; 3. Jaisalmer; 4. Golconda; 5. Bijapur; 6. Raigad

Page 38: 1. Burnside; 2. Wellington; 3. Mackintosh; 4. Jacuzzi; 5. Shrapnel; 6. Cardigan; 7. Leotard; 8. Sandwich

Page 39: 1. b; 2. a; 3. f; 4. e; 5. g; 6. d; 7. c

Page 40: 1. fossil fuels, shaped; 2. lightweight; 3. Leo Baekeland, decades; 4. landfills, ocean, biodegrade; 5. microplastics, swallow; 6. plant-based, bioplastic

Page 41: 1. Dhanbad; 2. Kanyakumari; 3. Dhaka; 4. Ahmedabad; 5. Howrah; 6. Amritsar; 7. Bhubaneswar; 8. Mysore

Page 42-43:

	Company 1	Company 2	Company 3
	Oral B	**Netflix**	**Nike**
Problem Statement 1	9. Children use their palms rather than their fingers to grip toothbrushes.	3. Viewers spend too much time and effort while trying to watch a program or film.	6. Customers have a wide choice of footwear, since most shoes are the same.
Solution Statement 1	12. The company introduced 'squish gripper' brushes with wider and softer handles.	10. The company introduced options such as 'Skip Intro' and 'Because you watched', to reduce effort.	8. The brand added transparent panels that showcased wearers' socks, which was a fun and funky element.
Problem Statement 2	1. Children do not like to brush their teeth.	7. Too many options can confuse viewers with too much choice, and decision-making is a chore.	2. Sports footwear should aid, not hinder, the performance of the sportsperson.
Solution Statement 2	5. The design team used bright colours and engaging graphics to make children look forward to brushing their teeth.	4. The introduction of short trailer videos and the Shuffle button customized viewer preferences and improved user experience.	11. The company introduced pressurised air technology, which enhanced athletic performance.

Page 44-45: 1. languages; 2. flying car; 3. communicate; 4. DNA; 5. surgeries; 6. colonise; 7. body temperature; 8. minds

Page 46-47: 1. Port Blair; 2. Kerala; 3. Jaipur; 4. Kaziranga National Park; 5. Gulmarg; 6. Keoladeo National Park; 7. Patan; 8. Baliman Dara; 9. Goa; 10. Bandhavgarh National Park; 11. Bijapur; 12. Rishikesh

Page 48-49: 1. Visva-Bharati University; 2. Stanford University; 3. Oxford University; 4. Columbia University; 5. Yale University; 6. Cornell University; 7. Harvard University; 8. Tribhuvan University; 9. Nalanda University; 10. Cambridge University

Page 50-51: 1. b; 2. c; 3. d; 4. a; 5. h; 6. g; 7. f; 8. e

Page 52-53: 1. Batik; 2. Coffee; 3. Bauls; 4. Capoeira; 5. Flamenco; 6. Kalbelia; 7. Sbek Thom; 8. Truffle hunting; 9. Tango; 10. Dragon boat festival

Page 54-55: Across: 2. Galileo; 6. Apollo; 8. Luna 9; 9. Rakesh Sharma; 11. Columbia

Down: 1. John Glenn; 2. Gagarin; 3. Laika; 4. Mangalyaan; 5. Leonov; 7. Shepard; 10. Skylab

Page 56: 1. d; 2. c; 3. a; 4. e; 5. b; 6. h; 7. f; 8. g

Page 57: 1. Maulvi Ahmadullah Shah; 2. Veer Kunwar Singh; 3. Mangal Pandey; 4. Nana Saheb; 5. Rani Lakshmibai; 6. Bahadur Shah II

Page 58-59: **A.** 1. b. i 2. c. ii 3. a. iii 4. f. iv 5. d. v 6. e. vi

B. 1. TAYLOR SWIFT 2. KATY PERRY 3. SELENA GOMES 4. RIHANNA 5. ADELE 6. ED SHEERAN

C. 1. LOVESTORY 2. FIREWORK 3. CALM DOWN 5. LIFT ME UP 6. EASY ON ME 7. SHAPE OF YOU

Page 60: 1. c; 2. e; 3. g; 4. f; 5. a; 6. h; 7. d; 8. b

Page 61: 1. g; 2. e; 3. d; 4. b; 5. f; 6. a; 7. c

Page 62-63: 1. Madhya Pradesh; 2. Bihar; 3. Jammu and Kashmir; 4. Odisha; 5. Tamil Nadu 6. Andhra Pradesh; 7. Chhattisgarh; 8. Assam; 9. Karnataka; 10. Rajasthan; 11. Maharashtra; 12. Kerala

Page 64-65: 1. d; 2. c; 3. a; 4. b; 5. g; 6. h; 7. f; 8. e

Page 66-67: Across: 3. Animation; 6. Subtitles; 8. Dolby; 9. Berlin

Down: 1. Dadasaheb Phalke; 2. Toy Story; 4. Talkie; 5. Silent; 7. Lumiere

Page 68-69: 1. c; 2. a; 3. d; 4. b; 5. g; 6. e; 7. h; 8. f

Page 70-71: 1. e; 2. a; 3. d; 4. c; 5. b; 6. h; 7. j; 8. g; 9. f; 10. i

Page 72: 1. INS Vikramaditya; 2. INS Sahyadri; 3. INS Chakra; 4. INS Savitri; 5. Sindhu; 6. INS Talwar; 7. INS Beas; 8. INS Khukri

Page 73: 1. Ponta Delgada, Portugal; 2. Bergamo, Italy; 3. Portugal; 4. Nagpur, India; 5. Italy; 6. Turkey; 7. Kathmandu, Nepal; 8. Liverpool, England; 9. Austria; 10. Dar es Salaam, Tanzania; 11. Maiquetia, Venezuela

Page 74: 1. b; 2. a; 3. g; 4. e; 5. f; 6. d; 7. c

Page 75: 1. a; 2. a; 3. b; 4. b; 5. a

Page 76-77: 1. d; 2. c; 3. f; 4. a; 5. b; 6. e; 7. k; 8. j; 9. l; 10. g; 11. i; 12. h

Page 78-79: 1. The Sound of Music; 2. Titanic; 3. Slumdog Millionaire; 4. Gandhi; 5. Schindler's List; 6. The Godfather; 7. Rain Man; 8. My Fair Lady; 9. Ben-Hur; 10. The Lord of the Rings: The Return of the King 11. Oliver!; 12. CODA

Page 80-81: 1. coins; 2. paper; 3. blockchain; 4. Bitcoin; 5. El Salvador; 6. blocks; 7. mining; 8. internet; 9. wallet, keys; 10. bubble, Tulip; 11. electricity, footprint

Page 82: 1. President of India, Rajya Sabha; 2. 543, Lok Sabha; 3. Vidhan Sabha; 4. Governor, legislative council; 5. legislative assembly; 6. five, six

Page 83: 1. spice islands; 2. Swahili, Arabic; 3. Portuguese, Persians; 4. Stone Town; 5. monkey; 6. coral reefs; 7. uncertain; 8. Freddie Mercury

Page 84-85: 1. Jim Laker; 2. Steffi Graf; 3. Jahangir Khan; 4. Just Fontaine; 5. Nadia Comăneci; 6. Sir Roger Bannister; 7. Sir Steve Redgrave; 8. Michael Phelps; 9. Jesse Owens

Page 86-87: 1. cuneiform; 2. *Epic of Gilgamesh*; 3. wheel; 4. cylinder seal; 5. Ziggurat of Ur; 6. Semitic; 7. Sargon, Levant; 8. Assyrians; 9. Babylon; 10. Hammurabi's Code; 11. Persians

Page 88-89: 1. T; 2. F; 3. T; 4. F; 5. F

Page 90-91: 1. *Ramlila*; 2. *Pandavani*; 3. *Nautanki*; 4. *Therukoothu*; 5. *Bhavai*; 6. *Dastangoi*; 7. *Tamasha*; 8. *Koodiyattam*; 9. *Yakshagana*; 10. *Jatra*

Page 92: 1. c; 2. a; 3. b; 4. e; 5. d

Page 93: 1. c; 2. f; 3. b; 4. a; 5. d; 6. e

Page 94-95: 1. T; 2. F; 3. T; 4. F; 5. T

Page 96-97: a. Tsar; b. St Petersburg; c. poor; d. Alaska; e. 1917; f. Vladimir; g. communism h. Joseph Stalin; i. Second; j. dog; k. USA, l. Cold War; m. Iron Curtain; n. Berlin Wall o. Russia; p. St *Petersburg*

Page 98: Quiz Yourself 1: 1. c; 2. a; 3. a; 4. b; 5. d; 6. a; 7. d; 8. b; 9. c; 10; a; 11. b; 12. c

Page 99: Quiz Yourself 2: 1. d; 2. a; 3. c; 4. a; 5. b; 6. c; 7. a; 8. c; 9. d; 10. b; 11. a; 12. d

Page 100: Quiz Yourself 3: 1. d; 2. c; 3. a; 4. d; 5. b; 6. c; 7. b; 8. a; 9. c; 10; b; 11. d; 12. c

Page 101: Quiz Yourself 4: 1. d; 2. c; 3. a; 4. b; 5. d; 6. b; 7. a; 8. c; 9. b; 10. d; 11. c; 12. a